THE IDEA OF A
SECULAR SOCIETY

AND ITS SIGNIFICANCE FOR
CHRISTIANS

UNIVERSITY OF DURHAM
PUBLICATIONS

THE IDEA OF A
SECULAR SOCIETY

AND ITS SIGNIFICANCE FOR
CHRISTIANS

―――

The Riddell Memorial Lectures
Thirty-fourth Series
delivered at King's College in the
University of Durham
on 13, 14, and 15 March 1962

BY

D. L. MUNBY
Fellow of Nuffield College, Oxford

LONDON
OXFORD UNIVERSITY PRESS
NEW YORK   TORONTO
1963

Oxford University Press, Amen House, London E.C.4

GLASGOW NEW YORK TORONTO MELBOURNE WELLINGTON
BOMBAY CALCUTTA MADRAS KARACHI LAHORE DACCA
CAPE TOWN SALISBURY NAIROBI IBADAN ACCRA
KUALA LUMPUR HONG KONG

PRINTED IN GREAT BRITAIN

CONTENTS

I

THE IDEA OF A SECULAR SOCIETY

NEARLY a quarter of a century ago, that most revolutionary and learned of modern poets, Mr. T. S. Eliot,
following an equally revolutionary and learned poet
a hundred years previously, produced a tract on *The
Idea of a Christian Society*, a tract as conservative in its
general temper and tone as its predecessor.[1] We may
suspect that his predecessor had the edge on Mr. Eliot
in the depth of his knowledge and experience of society
and public affairs and in the relevance of what he had to
say to the society of his day, though we may find the
poetry of Mr. Eliot more to our taste today than that of
Coleridge. When Coleridge wrote his tract *On the Constitution of the Church and State, according to the Idea
of Each*, neither Church nor State had been reformed;
the 'middle classes' and the industrialists, much less the
ordinary man, had not achieved significant political
power; the Victorian revival of religion was still to
burgeon and reintroduce the persecuting propensities of
former ages, before it died away in a new indifference;
population was to expand the size of the British community beyond anything anticipated or believed possible in former periods; standards of living were to rise
(for all people of whatever class) in ways undreamt-of;

[1] *The Idea of a Christian Society* (Faber & Faber, 1939). S. T.
Coleridge, *On the Constitution of the Church and State, according
to the Idea of Each* (1830) (references to 1852 ed.).

and technical progress in the fields of transport and communications were to unite the world as never before, and to make possible within and between communities a mobility unparalleled since the age of migrations.

When Mr. Eliot wrote a hundred years later, the (relative) stability and peace that had been achieved between 1850 and 1914 had been shattered by a disastrous world war as destructive as it was unexpected. Mr. Eliot wrote in expectation of another such war, which in fact broke out before his book was published. The 1930's were about as grim a period of misgovernment and missed opportunities as Britain has ever known. It is therefore not surprising that Mr. Eliot could write that 'the difference between the Idea of a Neutral Society (which is that of the society in which we live at present) and the Idea of a Pagan Society (such as the upholders of democracy abominate) is, in the long run, of minor importance'.[2] There were good grounds in the thirties for believing that 'neutral societies' were doomed to disappear before the crusading zeal of Communism and Fascism, as one such disappeared in the Spanish Civil War; the strongest grounds for such beliefs were to be found in the incompetence, credulity, and supineness of 'liberal' leaders, the exceptions being the vigour of Roosevelt, whose effective impact on the European scene was minimal before war broke out, and the suspect and outcast Churchill.

Nearly twenty-five years later, though the danger, should war break out, of physical destruction of what we regard as civilization is more real than it ever was in the thirties, and though Communism has vastly extended

[2] Op. cit., p. 9.

its power in the world, it is less easy to be pessimistic about the inherent possibilities of our society, however much we may detest the complacency and vulgarity of the Macmillan era in decline. In spite of the theological prophecies that a people without God will perish, in spite of the condemnations of moralists who point to the allegedly growing laxity of sexual morals and the supposed increase in neuroses, our society has shown signs of vigour that would hardly have been believed in the thirties. The Neutral Society has become more neutral, without as yet showing signs of becoming more aggressively 'pagan', at least in the Communist or Fascist/Nazi sense, in which Mr. Eliot may be supposed to have intended his phrase to be interpreted. We are settling down to a secular society, to which the Church seems to be acclimatizing itself as it has acclimatized itself to most previous forms of society. We may look on this process with cynicism; and the way in which the Church acclimatizes itself is in many respects a matter for shame and protest. But we can also look on this process as salutary, and it is on this that I want first to concentrate.

In its studies of the 'Christian Responsibility towards Areas of Rapid Social Change', the World Council of Churches, following leads from the 'under-developed' areas themselves, has stated that 'it is the duty of Christians, in co-operation with other citizens, to seek to build a neutral state'.[3] Asian Christians in 1957 specifically gave approval to the 'Neutral or Secular State' which 'does not identify itself with any one particular

[3] *The Common Christian Responsibility towards Areas of Rapid Social Change in Asia, Africa and Latin America* (World Council of Churches, Department on Church and Society, 1956), p. 36.

religion'.[4] In 1959 a world-wide conference on these issues stated:

In the countries of rapid social change, . . . there is some measure of religious pluralism and large portions of the population have been secularized. In these countries Christians should work for the development of a State which is neutral as between the various religions represented in it. Sometimes this is called a 'secular state', but this should be distinguished from a State which promotes 'secularism', or which is based upon dogmatically secularist assumptions.[5]

To demand a neutral or secular State is not the same as to encourage a secular society. But the secular society exists and flourishes in 'Western' societies, and is likely to develop in Communist societies as they grow to maturity and as Communist dogma becomes as irrelevant to the concerns of the common man as have the theological pretensions of the Christian Church in the West. It is time to count our blessings and to assess our heritage of secularism.

Our secular society may be seen as largely the product of the Christian West. With the possible exception of

[4] *Social Goals of New Asia* (East Asian Consultation (W.C.C.) at Pematang Siantar in 1957). Quoted in *The Witness of the Churches in the Midst of Social Change* (East Asian Christian Conference, 1959), p. 21.

[5] *Dilemmas and Opportunities: Christian Action in Rapid Social Change* (Report of an International Ecumenical Study Conference, Thessalonica, Greece, 25 July–2 August 1959) (W.C.C., Department on Church and Society, 1959), p. 45. The New Delhi Assembly of the W.C.C. stated that, though 'man cannot live as true man in a rootless world. He needs the structure of a society', yet 'it may also be that secularism is an essential element of culture in nations which have many religious communities' (*New Delhi Speaks* (S.C.M., 1962), p. 35).

some brief periods in the history of ancient Greece and of the Roman Empire in its hey-day, there have been few secular societies in the whole course of human development in the world. In most societies religion has been closely woven into the whole fabric of society, determining its structure and the pattern of men's ideas and goals; religious images have been dominant in men's imaginations and formed the focus of their culture in its widest sense. The dominance of religion has often meant the domination of priests and theologians, or the impositions of the ecclesiastical hierarchy. Disputes about power have become disputes about religious systems and still today such issues lurk behind many of our disputes within Europe, and between Europe and the rest of the world. But the pattern of historical development in Western Europe and those areas which derive their culture from it has been such as to distinguish between beliefs and practice and to separate the various departments of life from each other. It can be claimed that it is the peculiar glory of Western Christianity to have permitted such a development, however unintentional was its emergence. The cynic could, of course, counter-claim not without some justice that it only came about through exhaustion after the internecine wars between Christians, when the rest of the world lost patience with them.[6]

[6] But the process goes back long before the Enlightenment's reaction from the religious wars of the seventeenth century. Thus R. W. Southern writes of the twelfth century: 'Hildebert, and scholars who came after him, . . . were opening up a new vein of political theory, based on human rights and needs, and the innate dignity of the secular order of society. . . . They raised secular government from the dust of violence and self interest while they divested it of the cloak of a semi-priestly authority. . . . This process of limiting the scope of the appeal to the supernatural in human affairs had,

What are the marks of a secular society? No doubt there are many different aspects and I can but choose a few points of significance. These points provide a summary of today's practice. They reflect the idea of our society, an idea which is generally attacked by Christians. It is my purpose to suggest that, in so doing, they are wrong. What I say may, I suspect, at once appear obvious and perhaps at the same time improper and subversive.

X X (a) A secular society is one which explicitly refuses to commit itself as a whole to any particular view of the nature of the universe and the place of man in it. The State neither requires subscription to any particular doctrines nor overt forms of religious behaviour as a condition for claiming full rights as a citizen; furthermore, it does not in any significant sense attach itself to any church or religion. Clearly in Britain today the existence of two established churches, and the requirements of Biblical instruction in schools, as well as the favoured position of the established churches in the universities and the favoured position of all the Christian churches in the national broadcasting system, might be taken to suggest that Britain is not a secular society. In my view the significance of these facts can be greatly exaggerated. The establishment of the two churches in Britain is a vestigial survival of the past, of little practical importance. The place of religion in education is obviously of more moment, but in practice it does little to cover up the actual divergences of belief and behaviour, which

as its counterpart, a process of limiting the interferences of secular persons in spiritual affairs. . . . It was a symptom of a more refined spirituality which found something crude in the constant and automatic appeal to the supernatural in earthly matters' (*The Making of the Middle Ages* (Grey Arrow ed.), pp. 100–3).

are as evident in school, university, and broadcasting as in any other sphere of life.

We need to distinguish between a secular society and State. Society is wider than the State and its operations—even today. A Christian society could indeed exist with a secular State which did not express Christian beliefs in any organized way. But today we have certainly not got a Christian society. In effect, for most important purposes we are a secular society, where it makes little or no difference in what our religion or morality consists, and in which Christians are a small minority. That the State machinery continues to incorporate archaeological fragments appropriate to former periods when society was Christian is of less importance than the dominant mores of society.

In contrast with this view Mr. Eliot wrote:

You cannot expect continuity and coherence in politics, you cannot expect reliable behaviour on fixed principles persisting through changed situations, unless there is an underlying political philosophy: not of a party, but of the nation. . . . A positive culture must have a positive set of values. . . . It is only by returning to the eternal source of truth that we can hope for any social organisation which will not, to its ultimate destruction, ignore some essential aspect of reality.[7]

Continuity and coherence might indeed be found in a settled policy of open-mindedness to all views and respect for men in all their differences; but it would clearly not be the positive culture envisaged by Eliot. But what is interesting is how widespread, even among liberal Christians, who would not subscribe to the rigidities of Eliot's doctrines, is the view that the State

[7] Op. cit., pp. 40, 46, 63.

should in some sense openly espouse either the Christian faith or at least acknowledge belief in God. One can quote Alec Vidler for the liberal case for the establishment on the grounds that the State should recognize the Church 'on grounds of truth and not of expediency alone', and that the Church has a duty to bear witness to the nation (and against it, if required) to the true function of the State under God.[8] Even across the Atlantic, where we find the United States government acknowledging God, though with little, if any, Christian commitment, Professor John Bennett can write that 'there is no reason to move beyond the idea of a state that is neutral as between the great religious traditions to a state that is avowedly secular'.[9] The position in America is different from that in Britain in that there is a far more widely diffused religiosity—and indeed committed Christian practice also. There is not quite the same sharp contrast between those who openly accept the Christian faith and those who deny it or ignore it. Thus the liberal case for some sort of establishment or State acknowledgement of religion is perhaps stronger in the United States than in Britain. But the question remains whether even a liberal establishment

[8] *The Orb and the Cross* (1945), p. 94; *Christian Belief and This World* (1956), p. 45; *Essays in Liberality* (1957), pp. 101, 174 n.

[9] *Christians and the State* (1958), pp. 8–9. He goes on: 'I believe that a better approach in this country is to have it clearly understood that the state is neutral as between the traditional faiths, that it is not a secular state or indifferent to the religious life of the citizens or to the relevance of their religion to its affairs, that it does not *profess* a common-denominator religion, that it is in no sense a teacher of religion but that it does use symbols and provides for acts of religious recognition that refer to the Reality which the churches and other religious bodies alone are competent to interpret.' The book as a whole covers a wide field, of which this is only a small part.

of this kind does proper justice to those who do not regard it as truth, but rather humbug, to acknowledge God. In a world where only a minority are atheists, is it not the responsibility of the majority to go out of their way to respect them? It is not clear what would be positively lost, even in a society where a majority were Christian, if the State machinery scrupulously refused to concern itself with this fact.[10]

(b) Such a society is unlikely to be homogeneous, and we do not find homogeneity. Homogeneity could in theory arise spontaneously in such a society; in practice, the facts of past history which condition any society, the existence of division of labour on a large scale, the size of modern nations and the rate of economic growth (all facts relevant to the emergence of secular societies) make it extremely unlikely that homogeneity will arise spontaneously. A secular society is in practice a pluralist society, in so far as it is truly secular. Societies which enforce, whether by State coercion, or by social pressures, a uniform attitude of behaviour in important matters of human behaviour and values, whether or not these are regarded as religions, are in effect sacral societies of the traditional form, and not secular societies. Such was Nazi Germany, and such the pressures of social conformity in the United States (manifested in their extreme form in McCarthyism); though the United States is obviously a pluralist, secular society, there are strong pressures towards a traditional sacral form, though these manifest themselves in the activities of

[10] It is for this reason that I am not convinced by John Bennett's argument that 'we have to weigh the negative religious freedom of a small minority over against the positive religious freedom of the vast majority' (op. cit., p. 10), a point that is in general obviously valid.

psychiatrists, sociologists, politicians, local Rotary clubs, and other groups normally regarded as part of the 'secular world'.

Because a secular society is pluralist in many different ways there will be many people who find themselves under pressure in particular activities, jobs, or regions of the country which are dominated by the adherents of particular religions, or patterns of behaviour. Thus the protests of the so-called 'humanists' against religious domination of certain sectors of life (due largely to historical survival) should be regarded as one of the normal tensions of a secular society (which is not to justify the privileged position of Christians in these respects). Such tensions can and will occur in many other realms of society. Non-Presbyterians forced to work on Good Friday or Christmas Day in Scotland are subject to pressure. So often are Christians subjected to the dominant mores of doctors and psychiatrists. Non-Roman-Catholics may find themselves not always at ease in the Foreign Office, or those who disapprove of Puritanism in many parts of Wales and Scotland. Tensions, pressures, and attempts to dominate on the part of particular groups are part of life, and inevitable in a secular society. They are part of the price paid for variety and liberty.

It is one of the weaknesses of English society that it has never openly faced up to the actual divisions which exist within it, in contrast to the United States where they have forced attention to themselves, not indeed always with happy consequences. The history of State education provides some evidence of the divisions in Britain, but the final result is hardly one of which Christians can be proud. It fails to do justice to the actual divisions in our society, while at the same time the

continued existence of Anglican schools illustrates the
toughness of institutions more than any deeply felt con-
victions which require embodiment in a particular form
of education. There would seem to be a strong Christian
argument that the national acceptance of a limited place
for religion in State schools under the 1944 Act was
a disaster for the Church, in that it clouded over the real
division between Christians and non-Christians in our
country today and failed to face the realities of our
secular world. It may have been a triumph for religion;
was it a triumph for the Christian gospel? It is not at all
clear what objection there could be to a system of education which openly tried to allow for the real views of
particular groups in the community and to provide
means for their expression in special schools, if they so
desired it. If the State acted in this way as a provider of
the education desired by particular groups, there would
be no need for a dual system of education. But it would
involve a conscious acceptance of pluralism in education. Why should we not expect education to be as much
a sphere of divided beliefs and cultures as any other
realm of life?

By contrast to such an ideal we have Eliot's hankering
after a unified social code:

The unitary community should be religious–social, and
it must be one in which all classes, if you have classes, have
their centre of interest. . . . A Christian community is one in
which there is a unified religious–social code of behaviour.[11]

The justification of the existing system of education

[11] Op. cit., pp. 29, 34. Eliot does admit that a future Christian
society must be 'pluralist', following Maritain (p. 42), but he does
not give any content to this idea, except that his Community of
Christians will be 'a body of indefinite outline'.

seems to imply, though in attenuated form, the same ideal as does much other Christian thinking.[12] Is it not time that we faced the realities?

X X (c) A secular society is a tolerant society. It makes no attempt to enforce beliefs or to limit the expression of belief. Every society has to take action at those points where expression of belief is in effect a form of activity directed against the accepted policies of society, as for example in the various laws against incitement to disaffection, violence, or racial hatred. To draw the line between legitimate expression of belief and the undermining of the actual agreed policies of a given society is immensely difficult. But a stable secular society gives every benefit of doubt to the varied expression of belief, and is ready to incur risks in allowing their full manifestation.[13]

Likewise a secular society expressly tries to draw

[12] Coleridge, who believed firmly that the positive ends of government included 'the development of those faculties which are essential to his human nature by the knowledge of his moral and religious duties, and the increase of his intellectual powers in as great a degree as is compatible with the other ends of social union, and does not involve a contradiction. . . . Instruction is one of the ends of government' (*The Friend* (1844 ed.), II, p. 73), nevertheless deplored the education of the people being 'detached from the ministry of the Church' (*Church and State*, p. 72. See also p. 62, and *The Statesman's Manual—A Lay Sermon* (1870 ed. with *Biographia Literaria*), pp. 328 f.). That the complete secularization of education raises, in principle, great objections is not incompatible with the view that in practice since at least the early nineteenth century it has been utterly unrealistic to expect education to be provided except by the State.

[13] Thus the action of the authorities in using the Official Secrets Acts and similar heavy-handed measures against the Committee of 100 undermines confidence in our democratic institutions. However much one may deplore the rather childish methods of protest involved, the viewpoint held by supporters of C.N.D. deserves every serious consideration from those who disagree with it.

boundaries between public and private morality, and to widen the sphere of private decision and private choice. Thus Sir Patrick Devlin in his traditionalist lecture on *The Enforcement of Morals*[14] agreed that 'there must be toleration of the maximum individual freedom that is consistent with the integrity of society', but allowed that the presence of 'disgust' at some action 'is a good indication that the bounds of toleration are being reached'.

> We should ask ourselves in the first instance whether looking at it [homosexuality] calmly and dispassionately, we regard it as a vice so abominable that its mere presence is an offence. If that is the genuine feeling of the society in which we live, I do not see how society can be denied the right to eradicate it.

It is precisely the glory of a secular society that it does not allow our 'disgust' with the behaviour of others to lead to action against them. A secular society is one which tries to set bounds to the natural persecuting tendencies of human nature.

If a secular society is tolerant to the point where it consciously admits many different patterns of behaviour, some of which are held in abhorrence by other members of society, it cannot accept Mr. Eliot's view that:[15]

> The Christian can be satisfied with nothing less than a Christian organisation of society. . . . I do not see how it [the Church] can ever accept as a permanent settlement one law for itself and another for the world.

By contrast, Coleridge was an advocate of liberalism,

---

[14] From *Proceedings of the British Academy* (O.U.P. 1959), vol. xlv, pp. 17–18. [15] Op. cit., pp. 34, 95.

though his practical interpretation of his principles may have been more restrictive than we would like:[16]

It is a fundamental principle of all legislation, that the State shall leave the largest portion of personal free agency to each of its citizens, that is compatible with the free agency of all, and not subversive of the ends of its own existence as a State.

The crux of true liberalism today may be found in the field of marriage law. Too often discussion proceeds as if what were in question was the proper nature of marriage, and as if, once this had been decided, the nature of the law followed. Thus Christians rarely argue the case for a particular law in a world where people do not, as a matter of fact, live according to the Christian view of marriage. It is one thing to hold a high view of Christian marriage; it is another to insist that this should be the law of the land. It is one thing within the Christian community to legislate in a particular way; it is another thing to advocate laws for all and sundry. A properly pluralist view of society which treats other people with tolerance would be more ready to look critically at the accepted Christian position on the marriage laws. It might even be ready to accept varying kinds of marriage in one society; this again would be no more than the acceptance of the realities of the world in which we live. There is far more variety in customs and actual behaviour in different parts of the country and among different social groups than is normally recognized. To say this is not to justify easy divorce on moral grounds, but rather to do justice to the actual ways in which people prefer to live.

[16] Op. cit., p. 140.

(d) Any society must have some common aims, in the sense that people are doing things together to produce certain effects. The effects must be willed, or at least accepted. In order to produce these effects there must be organization, an agreed method of solving problems, and a common framework of law. There must be political institutions, a legal system, and an economic organization. The existence of these will produce their own momentum, and impose their own pattern on individual lives and social groups. They will determine the division of the national income into individual incomes, the patterns of hierarchy by which orders are given and received, and the distribution of rewards and punishments which stimulate and repress. No doubt their influence covers a wide area of human life. We are no doubt moulded by the way we earn our daily bread more deeply than we like to admit; we always have been and always will be.

But, granted all this, in a secular society these organizations and institutions have limited aims—at least in principle. No doubt Karl Marx was right when, in his grandiose prophetic vision of the glories and miseries of capitalism, he thus pictured it in the now hackneyed phrases:[17]

The bourgeoisie, wherever it has got the upper hand, has put an end to all feudal, patriarchal, idyllic relations. It has pitilessly torn asunder the motley feudal ties that bound man to his 'natural superiors', and has left remaining no other nexus between man and man than naked self-interest, than callous 'cash payment'. It has drowned the most

[17] Communist Manifesto (Marx and Engels, *Selected Works* (2 vols., 1950), vol. i, p. 35).

heavenly ecstasies of religious fervour, of chivalrous enthusi-
asm, of philistine sentimentalism, in the icy water of
egotistical calculation.

Christians have usually cheered the Marxists at this
point. But might we not turn this upside down and
assert that it is precisely the glory of modern society to
free men from the crushing burden of these so-called
'idyllic relations', and to limit the impositions of men
on each other to 'callous cash payment'? If the economic
order functions more or less efficiently, and more or less
justly, then the restriction of links between men to cash
payments frees them for the pursuit of their own aims
in a way that 'idyllic relations' do not.

The limited aims of a modern economic system are,
in principle, to increase the goods and services available
to people, which is to provide them with ever-widening
choices, and to make available to them the new products
which improved technology makes possible. That in fact
modern economic systems offer their rewards unequally
and unjustly, both within nations and as between
nations, does not contradict these principles, nor does
the remedy of these deficiencies require a totally new
economic system; more just systems of taxation and
more lavish economic aid from richer to poorer
countries can take account of these failures of justice
(though they do not in practice). Nor again does the
fact that the introduction of new products is accom-
panied by attempts by their sponsors to mould our tastes
and frighten and cajole us with the insistent blandish-
ments of advertising deny the possibility that a society
less dominated by the political power of these interested groups would know how to deal with them. In
principle, a modern economic system is a neutral system

for enlarging the choices of men and making available to them the powers of modern science. If we allow these powers to be misused, we are ourselves to blame.

Similarly, it is indeed natural that, given the existence of political and judicial institutions, those who have to operate them, like those who have to operate in other spheres of life, are tempted to magnify the importance of their particular contribution to society. We must allow to politicians the natural desire to make their humdrum role appear more grandiose than it really is; but we should not take their pretensions at their face value. They are often the victims of a hangover from the sacral society where the leaders of political life are also the leaders of society and the architects of manners and morals. The role of Mr. Macmillan is not that of Pericles, nor even perhaps that of Gladstone; and the sooner both sides recognize it the better. A secular society deflates the pretensions of politicians, but also the pretensions of judges, who vainly attempt to preserve some relics of their former role as prophet-priests of the national conscience. In principle, the functions of both law and politics are limited and specific in the kind of world in which we live, however much in practice we do not realize these aims. Here again, is not all this (at least potentially) great gain for the liberation of the human spirit? But do we not find resistance among Christians to full acceptance of its implications?

(e) In such a world we have discovered how various are the problems that can be solved by examination of the facts. Though we are often slow to make the full use of our opportunities, we do in fact in more and more directions determine policy through the prior analysis of the actual situation. It requires no great subtlety to point out that men do not always act with due regard to the facts, and that men's aims are not inhibited by such obstacles as their inability to achieve them or their lack of concordance with reality. It remains, nevertheless, surprisingly true that, in a large number of cases, once the facts have been elucidated, the appropriate action almost inevitably follows.[18] Our emotions and irrational impulses almost as often mislead us in our analysis of the situation as in the direction of our efforts; so that once we have received clear proof of the nature of a given situation, we are less inclined to knock our heads against a brick wall. There is no need to deny the importance of clashes between different people over matters of ethics, but even these are sometimes confused by disagreements about the facts. We like to buttress our moral arguments with factual premisses.[19]

[18] A classic example is the story of Chadwick and the public health movement in the nineteenth century, which is often portrayed as a struggle between the apostles of light and darkness. But a careful study of the evidence (see *The Life and Times of Sir Edwin Chadwick*, by S. E. Finer (1952)) suggests that disputes about the facts were often also much in issue. Chadwick's policies were based on the theory that 'All smell is disease' as against the rival view that diseases were caused by contagion. He believed in research and experiment, but he also clung dogmatically to his prejudices and tried to twist the evidence to suit them. He often found it easier to denounce his enemies rather than carefully assess the strength of their position. Not all the doctors and engineers who opposed him were suborned by vested interests. It is interesting that one of the few people who seemed to have kept his head and tried to assess the evidence was Palmerston (p. 457).

[19] A similar point has been made by Mr. Alasdair MacIntyre ('A Society without a Metaphysics', *Listener*, 13 Sept. 1956). 'When theologians are considering the problems of divorce, for example, their argument nowadays has to be two-pronged. Divorce, they will suggest, is objectionable both because it increases human unhappiness and because it violates the divinely ordained harmony of marriage. I am not in the least concerned here with the rights and

In the field of overall social policy, the use of study of the facts has a rather wider application. One of the most important sets of facts about which we need to know are the actual aims, intentions, impulses, and motivations of the various groups in society. Such knowledge may serve the cynical purposes of those who control public opinion or wish to control the destinies of other people. But it is equally necessary in order that, in a complex society, men may be able, as far as possible, to achieve the aims and intentions they set themselves. The liberal secular society, by contrast with most previous societies, does not set itself any overall aim, other than that of assisting as fully as possible the actual aims of its members, and making these as concordant with each other as possible. If a society gives itself an aim defined by its leaders or by its high-priests or intelligentsia, then it only needs to know enough to ensure that its dogmas

wrongs of divorce. What I want to bring out is how fatal the use of this type of argument must be to theology; fatal because one prong of the argument transforms the theologian into a social scientist and the other preserves his theology at the cost of making it humanly irrelevant for most people.' I am not convinced that the second prong is indeed as fatal as is here alleged.

That theologians do in fact use this two-pronged argument can be illustrated from the highest authority, the former Archbishop of Canterbury (*Problems of Marriage and Divorce* (S.P.C.K.) 1955)). The theory that marriage is a contract, he writes, 'by reducing the status of the home and family to a contract open to revision at will, disturbs and demoralizes society. It is repugnant to religion' (p. 7). 'The social evils springing from broken homes became the more evident as their number increased. In particular, evidence accumulated from all sides of the dreadful harm done to the children of broken homes' (p. 18). 'Broken homes' is used in relation to divorce, and, of course, obscures the issue as to how far divorce makes a home more 'broken' than it was before. 'It was that principle that the Church must uphold and secure today—not only as the true Christian principle but as vital, therefore, for the health and stability of the nation' (p. 19).

are realized in practice. In a simple society it can rely on tradition for guidance as to how these ideals may be realized; in a more differentiated society it will require specialized knowledge, but only enough to be able to manipulate people. But where it sets itself the aim of helping people to achieve their own aims, it requires more sensitive tools to make known what these aims are.

We owe in Britain an enormous debt to Bentham and the Utilitarians, and their successors. No doubt to set as the aim of society the greatest happiness of the greatest number is seriously to misunderstand the nature of human beings. To attempt to force upon them what a small group believes to be their proper happiness leads to the grossest tyranny, even if the leaders are as disinterested as Dostoievsky's Grand Inquisitor or as widely understanding of human impulses as we may perhaps expect in the future the best sociologists and psychologists to be. The Utilitarians often proved dictatorial in practice and their doctrines have been misused by those who wish to plan other people's lives for them. But it is not a large step from trying to make people happy to trying to help them to achieve the actual aims they set themselves. The history of the use of utilitarian ideas in economic theory shows how the criterion of maximizing utility ends up as the criterion of preference as actually manifested in the conduct of human beings in the market. The achievement of the Utilitarians was to place the emphasis on actual human beings as the constituents of society and their concrete desires as the ultimate justification of society's rules. Thus they were able to sweep away a great mass of mystification about rights and the ideal ends of society which enabled people to oppress others and to neglect their actual interests for the benefit of illusory abstractions. And so the utilitarian revolution laid the basis of a truly human secular society, in spite of the narrowness of utilitarian ideas of human nature.

In the economic field the development of a market economy which is consciously controlled by governments so as to avoid the disruptions to which a pre-Keynesian order was unavoidably subject, enables men to exercise their choices within the limits of the incomes they are permitted by society. Such freedom of choice within the market framework is, of course, by no means perfect in a world of advertising and monopolies; but in principle it can be improved, and by improvement we can widen the area of rationality and responsibility. The development of economic thinking and its successful application in practice has enabled us to produce some notable achievements in its limited field. The twentieth century may produce similar striking developments in the sociological and psychological fields— indeed it has already shown us something of what is possible, and we are slow to make use of what we know. The collection and study of economic facts is widely practised, but we are less advanced in the purely social fields.[20] The questionnaire and social survey can hardly

[20] It is peculiarly difficult for the British, as an American, Professor George Homans, wittily pointed out in a talk on 'Giving a Dog a Bad Name' (*Listener*, 16 Aug. 1956). 'Induction from observation suggests that Britons object to sociology—indeed, for them sociology *is* sociology—only if the creatures in question are alive, human, and British. . . . The British are enthusiastic students of the social behaviour of dead Britons. . . . The study of the customs of native tribes flourishes in Britain as it does in no other country. . . . My final and crucial test is that of the non-human Britons: the bird and the dog. Shamelessly, the British observe their social behaviour, not only in the field but in the home.' Having shown the folly of a

be expected to prove as sensitive tools for the recording of human desires as are the actual choices people make in the market when they spend their money; but they could enable us to go much farther in enabling people to achieve their aims, if we were ready to use them more fully and intelligently. It is perhaps regrettable that we do not always find Christians welcoming honest inquiry into the facts. Rather they often seem to fear them, in the spirit of Mr. Portpipe, though without his forth-rightness:[21]

Man has fallen, certainly, by the fruit of the tree of knowledge; which shows that human learning is vanity and a great evil, and therefore very properly discountenanced by all bishops, priests, and deacons.

(f) A secular society is a society without official images. If there are no common aims, there cannot be a common set of images reflecting the common ideals

---

number of the explanations given as to why the British dislike sociology, Homans seems to conclude that the fundamental factor is the pressure of other academic subjects in universities. 'In spite of all objections, a great and increasing amount of sociology is being done in Britain. But it tends to be done in research institutions, not as part of a regular university programme; or, if in universities, then in London and the provinces, not in Oxford or Cambridge; or, if in Oxford and Cambridge, not under the name of sociology.' There is a good deal of truth in this.

[21] *Melincourt*, by T. L. Peacock. (*The Novels*, ed by David Garnett (1948), p. 199.)

We may compare F. D. Maurice's description of the religion of his day (*Life*, ed. by his son F. Maurice (1885), vol. i, p. 441): 'For the steadfastness of Balaam in refusing to turn aside when the creature on which he rode refused to go forward, is precisely the steadfastness of our country gentlemen, be they High or Low Church-men, and false prophets. They do not believe that facts are angels of the Lord, saying "Thus far shalt thou go and no farther".'

and emotions of everyone. Nor can there be any common ideal types of behaviour for universal application. Former societies glorified certain occupations, no doubt reflecting the class structure of particular epochs. All could not aspire to become monks or knights, but in a small highly-structured society such ideals were perhaps not entirely without relevance to everyday life in the Middle Ages. But today in a society of large size and enormous variety there can be no such ideal patterns of life. Nor can there be any common images to coordinate and focus our disorderly emotions. It is perhaps not surprising that in such a society the only common image we can find is one so vacuous and tawdry as the Royal Family; it is however surprising when we find men of sense and intelligence pretending that the Royal Family provides a deep emotional focus for our community.

It is not merely that in a large-scale society such ideals and images would prove difficult to focus. In such a society they are out of place. There is no image or ideal of the Common Man in the age of the Common Man. The Common Man is you or I following our particular jobs with our particular aims and ideals, and neither you nor I should attempt to do the job of each other, nor do we do ourselves justice if we merely copy others. A liberal society (and it is to be remembered that I speak of the ideal) does not expect the common man to ape his betters. That is appropriate for the age of the few, who lord it over others, not for the age of the many. Nor does it expect us all to have the same values and impose them on others. It respects our variety, and cannot therefore countenance any accepted images and ideals.

It is perhaps not surprising that it is as poet and critic

that Eliot writes: 'You cannot expect continuity and coherence in literature and the arts, unless you have a certain uniformity of culture.' So again he deplores 'the absence of any common background of knowledge'.[22] There is indeed a problem for poets and artists, and it is not surprising that a society such as ours finds them divided into what seem to outsiders to be narrow cliques, nor is it surprising that the characteristic forms of art are abstract and expressionist. But it may be questioned whether we can ever again expect the coherent and common images of former ages.

In thus describing the idea of a secular society, I describe certain clear tendencies and partial achievements of the world in which we live. That we have been moving in this direction since the decline of Victorian religiosity could hardly be doubted. That many regard such a society as ideal can again hardly be doubted. It has not escaped comment that descriptions such as mine are negative, in that they point more to differences from previous societies and to the absence of traditional restraints than to anything positive. This is inevitably the case, given the nature of what is at stake. The positive aims of a sacral society, whether traditional or modern totalitarian, can be stated fairly simply. There are almost by definition no positive aims of a liberal secular society. But this is not to say that no positive ideals animate these rather negative aims.[23]

[22] Op. cit., pp. 38, 40.

[23] To say this is not to argue for *laissez-faire*, nor to set any particular limits on State action in the economic field. It is not a programme for political or economic Liberalism. State action in these fields has to be treated on its merits, which have little to do with the lack of overall positive aims of society.

The positive ideals that lie behind the idea of the secular society are firstly a deep respect for the individual man and the small groups of which society is made up. It is because we have such respect that we seek not to impose on others, and not to lord it over others. Thus the equality of all men, in some sense, is a positive ideal towards which we aim. With equality goes, as Daniel Jenkins has so clearly expressed in his *Equality and Excellence*,[24] an ideal that each man should be helped to acquire his peculiar excellence. An equal society in this sense does not mean a society which levels down (or up for that matter), but a society which respects each man's particular contribution. Being a growing society, it is one which tries continually to enlarge the opportunities open to all men. Respecting all men, it continually breaks down the traditional barriers of class and caste which hinder some groups from making their full contribution. To sum up, it is therefore because of respect for men that a secular society limits the common aims and ends of society as a whole. This is not because it accepts that men do not require organizations and social groupings to enable them to fulfil themselves, but because it believes that society as such exists for men, and not vice versa.

Two questions then arise. First, is such a society stable? Can it survive with the loose structure that is implied in the ideal? Or is it only because it feeds on the fast-disappearing organic realities of pre-industrial sacral society? Does it depend on the survival of the traditional mores and loyalties, which it proceeds to disintegrate? Secondly, can there be a neutral society which does not lapse, as Mr. Eliot implied, into some form of

[24] S.C.M. Press, 1961.

conscious paganism? Or, to put it another way, is such a society desirable from a Christian standpoint?

It is with some of the implications of these questions that I am concerned. It may be worth briefly sketching some of the conclusions, First, it would appear that modern society is more flexible than its critics allow, more capable of meeting disastrous changes, and in general more adaptable than previous societies. Precisely because it sets no common aims for itself, and because it exists in a world of rapid change, it is less brittle than static societies and more ready to meet new challenges than societies with rigid aims. The dangers of such a society as ours are not to be found in their likely failure to meet human needs, but rather in their meeting them too well. The dangers are not of disintegration but of inanity and boredom. It is the acceptance of the tawdry and second-rate and the complacency of those who are content that they have never had it so good which we should fear. If society as a whole has no aims, there may be little to spur men on to further achievements, and we may fail to attain the good we could achieve because we are so conscious that we do better than we did yesterday.

Second, there is no reason for Christians to complain. Such a society is framed more nearly in accordance with the Will of God as we can see it in Scripture, in the Incarnation, and in the way God actually treats men, than those societies which have attempted to impose on the mass of men what a small Christian group have believed to be in accordance with God's Will. Fortunately, the churches have been compelled by the impact of outside events to realize the errors into which they have fallen in the past. That there is a simplicity in the older view which disappears in the newer is not in doubt. Nor has the reformation of the churches come willingly, or even completely. But that what we are forced to learn is not contrary to the Will of God is not, in my view, to be doubted. But has this fact been generally accepted by Christians?

II

CHANGE, SPECIALIZATION, AND HUMAN VALUES

IN his tract *On the Constitution of the Church and State*, Coleridge distinguished two major aims of the State, to which corresponded two interest groups, namely 'The first of the two great paramount interests of the social state, that of permanence', and 'the other great interest of the social state, namely, its progressive improvement'. As he later put it, 'the two antagonist powers or opposite interests of the State, under which all other state interests are comprised, are those of permanence and of progression'. Permanence was represented by the landed interest, whereas 'all advances in civilisation, and the rights and privileges of citizens, are especially connected with, and derived from, the four classes, the mercantile, the manufacturing, the distributive, and the professional'.[1] But these two interests alone were deficient without 'the third great venerable estate of the realm', the national Church whose object was 'to secure and improve that civilisation, without which the nation could be neither permanent nor progressive'. Permanence and progressiveness 'depend on a continuing and progressive civilisation', but 'the ground, the necessary antecedent condition' of both is to be found in the third interest. And so Coleridge asserts the need for his 'clerisy' in the classic sentences:[2]

[1] pp. 15, 26, 28.   [2] pp. 50–52.

Civilisation is itself but a mixed good, if not far more a corrupting influence, the hectic of disease, not the bloom of health, and a nation so distinguished more fitly to be called a varnished than a polished people, where this civilisation is not grounded in cultivation, in the harmonious development of those qualities and faculties that characterise our humanity. We must be men in order to be citizens.

The inspiration Coleridge provided for many Christian social thinkers has been deep and continuous up to our times. The scheme I have just outlined provides a framework for a just appreciation of the roles of the present-day Tory and Labour Parties; it can also serve as a guide to the major problems of our day. The questions we need to raise are, firstly, whether the interests of permanence have not been subordinated to those of progress, or whether the commercial interest, as Coleridge himself warned in his writings, has not predominated so as to produce 'the hectic of disease'; secondly, whether in our progressive, specialized, and splintered society we have not ceased to be 'men', and are therefore incapable of being 'citizens'.

As to the first question, it would seem that modern Christian followers of Coleridge have laid excessive stress on the need for permanence and ignored the proper analysis of progress. This is perhaps not surprising in so far as they have been of conservative temper, if not Tory in politics. Coleridge himself presented a far more balanced view, which allowed both for the expansion of the national income by the activities of businessmen and also for the welfare role of the State to redress these activities by spreading their benefits more widely. Thus he asked, 'Is the increasing number of wealthy individuals that which ought to be understood by the wealth of the nation?' and clearly answered that 'the wealth of the nation (that is, of the wealthy individuals thereof), and the magnitude of the revenue [were] mistaken for the well-being of the people'.[3]

Similarly Coleridge held the eighteenth-century (and modern Keynesian) view that government expenditure was a stimulating force in the economy:[4]

Does not war create or re-enliven numerous branches of industry as well as peace? . . . Does not this, like all other luxury, act as a stimulus on the producing classes, and this in the most useful manner, and on the most important branches of production, on the tiller, on the grazier, the clothier, and the maker of arms? . . .

To what can we attribute this stupendous progression of national improvement, but to that system of credit and paper currency, of which the national debt is both the reservoir and the water-works?

In many details the exposition of this view would not be acceptable today;[5] but it is nearer to the truth than the

---

[3] Op. cit., pp. 75, 77.

[4] *The Friend* (1844 ed.), vol. ii, pp. 40, 46–47. The whole Essay III is entitled 'On the Vulgar Errors respecting Taxes and Taxation'. It was circulated in November 1809 (see J. Colmer, *Coleridge: Critic of Society* (1959), p. 112).

[5] While Coleridge is fundamentally right in what he says about expenditure, he is not always clear that it is spending which produces the favourable results. He assumes that taxation is spent by the government (a not unreasonable assumption in his day) and thereby skates over the depressing effect of taxation in so far as it reduces private consumption. He also seems to believe that the very existence of the national debt is a good thing, rather than the government spending which has led to its increase. Thus he can say that 'it is the national debt which has wedded in indissoluble union all the interests of the state, the landed with the commercial, and the man

'vulgar errors' which Coleridge attacked, and which became the dominant dogmas of the classical economists and of Victorian financial practice. Coleridge is concerned with unemployment[6] and the national output, and uses the image of an irrigation system to illustrate 'the dispersion of that capital through the whole population, by the joint effect of taxation and trade'.[7]

It is also notable that, in his second *Lay Sermon*, published in 1817, in addition to further remarks on unemployment, government expenditure, and similar matters, he outlined a view of the credit cycle (as the trade cycle was known in the nineteenth century) which was very modern, if not unusual, for the date.[8] Coleridge was not averse to detailed discussions of economic matters, in which what he said was not simply foolish, as is all too often the case today with those who write from similar backgrounds. He did indeed too easily slip from the analytical to the moral, and from the contemporary to the eternal.[9] But he always remained a man of wide

of independent fortune with the stirring tradesman and reposing annuitant' (pp. 44–45).

[6] pp. 48, 60.   [7] p. 39.

[8] *A Lay Sermon addressed to the Higher and Middle Classes, on the existing Distresses and Discontents* (1817), pp. 397 f., 424–7 (edition of 1870, together with *Biographia Literaria*). See also R. J. White, *Political Tracts of Wordsworth, Coleridge and Shelley* (1953), which reprints much of it and notes the freshness of his views on the trade cycle.

[9] e.g. 'A nation, of which the government is an organic part with perfect interdependence of interests, can never remain in a state of depression thus produced, but by its own fault, that is, from moral causes' (p. 397 n.). Later he found the 'true seat and sources' of 'the existing distress' in 'the overbalance of the commercial spirit' (p. 402). But the basic fact remains that the cure of the trade cycle came about only when Keynes developed his full analysis of the causes of unemployment.

knowledge of contemporary events in contrast to our modern poets.[10]

That his views were not more widely known was perhaps due more to the manner of their publication than to their obscurity. In his own journalistic endeavours (notably *The Friend*) and in his tracts, such as the *Lay Sermons*, we find a mass of rather heterogeneous material, not always very well ordered, and hardly conducive to persuading his readers.[11] It is no doubt because of this that his wide learning and grasp of subjects well outside what might be expected have been insufficiently recognized and his thought treated as that of a cloudy and obscure metaphysician, of little practical importance. This is the picture we find in Byron writing in 1818:[12]

> And Coleridge too, has lately taken wing,
> But like a hawk encumber'd with his hood,—

[10] Coleridge was for some years secretary to the Governor of Malta, and, as part of his duties, wrote briefs on the topics of the day. In these, as in his leaders for the *Morning Post*, he wrote clearly, concisely, and to the point, showing a mastery of detail and a common-sense approach, appropriate to a civil servant and journalist. (See Colmer, op. cit.)

[11] Coleridge's views on economic matters have been unduly neglected. Historians of economic thought have rarely looked at them, for obvious reasons, and others have not been interested. There is a reference to his views on government expenditure and war in D. H. Macgregor's *Economic Thought and Policy* (Home University Library (1949), p. 177), with a similar quotation from the classical economist McCulloch. There is no reference in an article which covers this field explicitly, though confining attention to what might be called professional economists (B. A. Corry, 'The Theory of the Economic Effects of Government Expenditure in English Classical Political Economy' in *Economica*, Feb. 1958). Coleridge may well have got his views from Lauderdale, who held similar views on the national debt. The well-known influence of Coleridge on John Stuart Mill was in the general field of social ideas (see e.g. Erich Roll, *A History of Economic Thought* (1945 ed.), pp. 358–9).

[12] *Don Juan*, Canto I, ii (written 1818, published 1819).

Explaining metaphysics to the nation—
I wish he would explain his Explanation.

The picture has been immortalized in Peacock's novels, where Coleridge apears as Mr. Panscope, Mr. Mystic, Mr. Flosky, and Mr. Skionar.[13] But the myth bears little relation to the man who emerges from his writings. The admiration Coleridge inspired in Mill did not extend to his economics. 'In political economy especially he writes like an arrant driveller, and it would have been well for his reputation had he never meddled with the subject.'[14] But this judgement was inspired by the dogmatic views held by the classical economists on the subject of the impossibility of 'over-production', rather than by careful analysis.[15] Today, after Keynes, we would be more charitable.

More important to our purpose than his analysis of government expenditure and employment is his recognition of 'the humanizing influences of commerce and reciprocal hospitality'.[16] 'As there are two wants connatural to man, so are there two main directions of human activity . . . trade and literature. . . . Without

[13] In *Headlong Hall, Melincourt, Nightmare Abbey*, and *Crotchet Castle* respectively. Mr. Mystic tells his companions (satirizing Coleridge's *Lay Sermons*) that 'General discontent shall be the basis of public resignation! The materials of political gloom will build the steadfast frame of hope' (*Novels*, ed. David Garnett (1948), p. 280).

[14] *Dissertations and Discussions* (1867), vol. i, p. 452, quoted by Roll, op. cit., p. 359.

[15] See e.g. T. W. Hutchison, *A Review of Economic Doctrines, 1870–1929*, pp. 348 f. S. G. Checkland ('The Propagation of Ricardian Economics in England', *Economica*, Feb. 1949) refers to Coleridge's failure to realize that Malthus's views were allied to his own in his dispute with the New Political Economy, but does not refer specifically to his views on gluts and expenditure (pp. 41–42).

[16] *The Friend*, vol. ii, p. 92.

trade and literature, mutually commingled, there can be no nation; without commerce and science, no bond of nations.' He did indeed believe, as we have seen, that if 'the commercial relations' were not 'under the ascendancy of the mental and moral character' there would result 'sooner or later . . . the fall or debasement of the country itself'. But it is perhaps surprising enough that a poet should show such an awareness of the importance of trade.[17]

Most important of all is that he regarded the hope of advancement as a right of all men. 'Our Maker has distinguished man from the brute that perishes, by making hope first an instinct of his nature, and, secondly, an indispensable condition of his moral and intellectual progression. . . . But a natural instinct constitutes a right, as far as its gratification is compatible with the equal rights of others.' He went further in asserting that 'the National Church' was 'the especial and constitutional organ and means' concerned to assure two ends of the State, namely, 'to secure to the subjects of the realm, generally, the hope, the chance of bettering their own or their children's condition', and 'to develop in every native of the country those faculties . . . which are necessary to qualify him for a member of the State'. The Church has indeed concerned itself with education, but do we not find it rather strange to read Coleridge saying that, in achieving the first end, the Church had found 'a most powerful surrogate and ally . . . in her former wards and foster-children, that is, in trade, commerce, free industry, and the arts'?[18] There have been many books pointing out how few have been the contacts

[17] *The Friend*, vol. iii, pp. 193–4.
[18] *Church and State*, pp. 83–85.

between the Church and the working-class movement; there have been few pointing out how limited have been its contacts with the world of businessmen.

Coleridge recognized that we live in a dynamic society, where the forces of change are indeed built in, in a world where scientists use their minds to discover new truths, technologists apply them to practical purposes, and the public likes to use the new inventions. It is worth repeating that in the last resort the new inventions are not mere gadgets, which only amuse and cajole, but, at least in the case of those which survive the fashions of a few years and make their deepest impact on human life, are really capable of enlarging men's opportunities and responsibilities.[19] Electricity, the telephone, wireless, television, the motor-car, the aeroplane, the electronic computer, the washing-machine, the camera, the tape-recorder, the deep-freeze—the list could go on—all assist the truly human purposes of men, enlarge our imaginations, reduce the amount of brute effort, and set us free for wider human contacts. Of course we abuse them and misuse them. But it can hardly be disputed that the world is a better place with them than without them. (One must indeed except the few who, in the past, could obtain many of the benefits afforded by the new inventions through the exploitation of the labour of large numbers of other people; for those who could call on the services of a large class of domestic servants the benefits are less than to most men, but these were always a very small class.) Nor can we seriously maintain that these new 'gadgets', as we sometimes contemptuously call them, are merely the products of aggressive advertising, which we are unwillingly cajoled into using. The

[19] See *God and the Rich Society* (1961), for further discussion of this.

businessman is a necessary and important link between the ultimate discoveries of the scientist (and their application by the technologist) and, on the other hand, the ordinary day-to-day user. But in the longer term, however much we put up with the excesses of commercialized advertisement in spheres where it is inappropriate, the 'gadgets' survive on their merits, because they serve the needs of men, and because men look to 'the hope of advancement'.

One of the most dubious, as well as the most serviceable, of our new inventions is the ubiquitous motor-car. Its advantages to the individual and the family require little elaboration, though one occasionally finds superior persons who appear to regard these as negligible. But the appalling problems the motor has brought in its train have certainly not been faced, much less treated. It is not merely the dreadful casualty rate, but, perhaps more serious in the long run, the destruction of the amenities of city and village life. Readiness to spend more on roads can avoid some of the destruction of amenities and eliminate some of the causes of accidents. But, in addition to this, discipline is required in such matters as speed-limits, pedestrian-crossings, and, more important, the limitation of the use of cars in cities so that shopping and other central areas can be restored to the pedestrian. This requires economic measures in the way of making the motorist pay the cost of the space he uses in parking and adding to traffic congestion, planning measures to limit access to certain areas, and investment in rebuilding city centres in new ways. It is indeed a failure of our civilization that we all expect to own and use cars, and at the same time are not ready to face up to the restrictions that universal ownership must impose on each of us unless life is to be hell for all. The motor-car requires social, economic, and political action, because a man cannot possess and use a car without effects on others. It is therefore a case where we can rightly expect political leadership of a kind we do not find. It is also notably a field where more research into facts and the application of their results would produce large dividends.[20] It is the clearest example of the ambiguous nature of technical progress. But we must still remember that people do in fact find the car serviceable and that it does in fact widen the horizons of many. It is also true that we *could* do much to remove its disadvantages.

With these built-in forces of change, we need to look at the ways in which such a society as ours reacts to these changes. Mr. Eliot argues:[21]

My thesis has been, simply, that a liberalised or negative condition of society must either proceed into a gradual decline of which we can see no end, or (whether as a result of catastrophe or not) reform itself into a positive shape which is likely to be effectively secular. . . . Unless we are content with the prospect of one or the other of these issues, the only possibility left is that of a positive Christian society.

This statement, though more dogmatic than many, is not un-typical of many made by Christian apologists. If we ask why the alternatives should be so stark, Mr. Eliot tells us that it is because:

a negative culture has ceased to be efficient in a world

[20] Notable work is done in the Road Research Laboratory of the Department of Scientific and Industrial Research; but funds are inadequate and its results are not applied as much as they could be.

[21] Op. cit., pp. 25, 13, 16.

where economic as well as spiritual forces are proving the efficiency of cultures which, even when pagan, are positive.

Or, more generally,

By destroying traditional social habits of the people, by dissolving their natural collective consciousness into individual constituents, by licensing the opinions of the most foolish, by substituting instruction for education, by encouraging cleverness rather than wisdom, the upstart rather than the qualified, by fostering a notion of *getting on* to which the alternative is a hopeless apathy, Liberalism can prepare the way for that which is its own negation: the artificial, mechanised or brutalised control which is a desperate remedy for its chaos.

Mr. Eliot might be less pessimistic today, when liberal societies have been shown to possess reserves of efficiency unsuspected in the thirties. But he might be able to pinpoint more sharply the vices of a lower-middle-class society addicted more intensely than pre-war to 'getting on' and to the 'artificial' and 'mechanised' culture-substitutes provided by some of its leaders.

The case against a secular society is then that it undermines the cultural values without which men cannot remain permanently satisfied. It uproots men from their traditional stabilities, demands of them a rationality they cannot bear, and continuously disassociates them from their fellow men, as the changing social and economic forces break up any groupings, whether regional or professional, at work, or in the places where people live, almost as soon as they are able to form them. In place of the satisfactions given by these stable and traditional groups, it dangles before men, so it is asserted, the meretricious and ultimately unsatisfying hopes of riches or status, hopes which cannot be satisfied because only a few can have vastly more riches or status than others. Such societies seem to their critics to produce a state of permanent neurosis, which must ultimately lead to graver catastrophe. The price to be paid for riches is to be tied to machines; the price to be paid for the search for status is to be forced to conform to patterns of spending and living determined by advertisers and aped by one's neighbours. Far from being enriched by the new powers, men become the slaves of new and more compelling social and economic processes. Such is the case for the prosecution.

One difficulty with the general argument is the lack of precision about terms such as 'decline', 'catastrophe', 'chaos'.[22] If we are referring to what happened in Spain or Czecho-Slovakia in the thirties or to the Congo after the departure of the Belgians, such terms have meaning. But it is not clear that it is always such events that the pessimists have in mind. Sometimes these phrases are used in such a prophetic manner that any actual set of events could be said to confirm the implied prediction. If we try to look backwards, we could ask whether, comparing the nineteen-fifties and sixties with the eighteen-twenties and thirties, we find the latter period 'diseased'; if we answer 'Yes', it is clear that the patient has not in any significant sense moved nearer to 'death'. In other words, in terms of this comparison, 'disease' is a phenomenon which does not preclude many particular desirable developments in society and does not rule out

[22] See Eliot, op. cit., pp. 16, 25. We have quoted above Coleridge on 'disease'. It is perhaps odd that we have to ask these questions of Mr. Eliot, who has always laid such stress on precision in language.

a situation which many people would think immensely better than the less diseased one. Similarly, if we compared the fifties or sixties with the twenties and thirties of this century, it is not at all clear that we are in any unambiguous or generally agreed sense 'worse off'. I am not sure, however, whether this can be taken as proof that Mr. Eliot was simply 'wrong' in what he was saying in 1939.

The major issue is whether 'commerce' has not gained too much predominance over 'literature' and 'science'. Put like this, we might well want to answer 'Yes', while agreeing that a vulgar commercialized society can flourish and meet many of the lower needs of men, without satisfying them in the more important matters. Such a society might be highly stable and successful as a society, without the men in it living lives of any great significance or value. It is indeed on these lines that we ought to criticize our society. But, being in principle a neutral secular society, it is up to the critics to show forth in practice a better way of life which could be lived within our opportunities. It is not so clear that there is anything inherent in the structure of our society which would prevent them so doing.

The arguments on both sides are indeed to be found expressed with admirable clarity and prescience by John Stuart Mill, in his 1840 essay on Coleridge already quoted:[23]

It might be plausibly maintained that in almost every one of the leading controversies, past or present, in social philosophy, both sides were in the right in what they affirmed, though wrong in what they denied; and that if

[23] *Dissertations and Discussions* (1867), vol. i, pp. 399–401.

either could have been made to take the other's views in addition to its own, little more would have been needed to make its doctrine correct. Take for instance the question how far mankind have gained by civilization. One observer is forcibly struck by the multiplication of physical comforts; the advancement and diffusion of knowledge; the decay of superstition; the facilities of mutual intercourse; the softening of manners; the decline of war and personal conflict; the progressive limitation of the tyranny of the strong over the weak; the great works accomplished throughout the globe by the co-operation of multitudes: and he becomes that very common character, the worshipper of 'our enlightened age'. Another fixes his attention, not upon the value of these advantages, but upon the high price which is paid for them; the relaxation of individual energy and courage; the loss of proud and self-relying independence; the slavery of so large a portion of mankind to artificial wants; their effeminate shrinking from even the shadow of pain; the dull unexciting monotony of their lives, and the passionless insipidity, and absence of any marked individuality, in their characters; the contrast between the narrow mechanical understanding, produced by a life spent in executing by fixed rules a fixed task, and the varied powers of the man of the woods, whose subsistence and safety depend at each instant upon his capacity of extemporarily adapting means to ends; the demoralizing effect of great inequalities in wealth and social rank; and the sufferings of the great mass of the people of civilized countries, whose wants are scarcely better provided for than those of the savage, while they are bound by a thousand fetters in lieu of the freedom and excitement which are his compensations. . . . Yet all that is positive in the opinions of either of them is true.

One part of the charge against our society is that it cannot survive because of the discords it inevitably produces. A rapidly changing and dynamic society, such as we have in the Western world, will indeed suffer from strains and conflicts. They will never cease; there is, after all, no limit to the possibilities of differences between men. But it is not so clear that these conflicts must inevitably produce such instability as will result in political or social chaos. The mere existence of the conflicts may indeed prevent disaster. If society has a stable pattern, whether simple or complex, but such as to limit particular groups to a fixed position in the social order, it is not surprising that the ferment of discontent with their position within any group will produce at best a totally new social order, at worst a period of conflict and disorder. But it is not like this in a social order whose pattern is itself fluid and perpetually changing. In such a society the principles of dynamic rather than static equilibrium apply.

A dynamic society, which is at the same time 'liberal' and 'open', does not require perfect adjustment at any given time. Totalitarian societies can indeed be dynamic, as Russian and Chinese experience has made abundantly clear. How far such societies will be forced to adapt their totalitarianism to the changes that their own dynamism brings about is not something that we can see clearly. But we *can* see fairly clearly the way in which a liberal society adjusts itself over the longer run to new conditions and conflicts, by producing a sort of moving equilibrium. It is absurd to argue that a highly democratic welfare society (even if it had got rid of the persistent class barriers of earlier ages and the excessive wealth of those at the top of the income ladder, which disfigure Britain and stimulate conflict) would be without other sources of conflict. A specialized large-scale society is a natural breeding-ground of conflict. To believe that there can be any ultimately successful techniques for solving conflicts or preventing them breaking out is to suffer from an extraordinary naïvety. But it is not entirely naïve to believe that an open dynamic society is more likely to adapt itself in such a way that these conflicts will not destroy it.

A democratic open society is one where pressure groups can exert influence on the seats of power and where large masses of men can vote for alternative leaders. The cynical claim of vulgar Conservative leaders such as Baldwin and Macmillan in decline that they give the people what they want is an abdication of the responsibilities of statesmanship, but it reflects the truth that in societies such as ours politicians cannot for long give the people what they positively do not want. Dealing in votes requires sensitiveness to the reactions of the public, and is some guarantee against social disintegration. It is not only in the political field that an open society allows men opportunities to adjust the social order to meet their frustrations. Pressures can also be exerted on the changing pattern of industry through trade-union action.[24] Perhaps most important of all is the fact that a society which is aware of the reality of continuous economic and social change, as well as of the possibilities of democratic political action, gives discontented groups hope that they will be able to alter conditions to their liking. It is when no such hopes remain that revolutions break out. Coleridge was right to lay such stress on men's hopes.

[24] The market itself also produces shifts in industrial power. Who would have foretold twenty (or even ten years) ago the present position of the coal industry?

That the conflicts are indeed real, acute, and by no means easy to solve can be illustrated in the case of two major contemporary issues in the economic and social fields. First, let me take a major economic conflict: I refer to the problem of wage–cost inflation and the demand for a national incomes policy. To analyse the problem in a general way is not difficult. If we are to continue with a full-employment economy, with 2 per cent. or less unemployment, which is more or less universally accepted as either a desirable first priority or at least a political necessity, then we have to face the danger of continually rising prices, with all the social and economic consequences which follow. In spite of the continuance of rising prices since the beginning of the war, we have not been near to the disaster of raging inflation which can, as the experience of Germany between 1919 and 1923 showed, destroy a social order more effectively than revolution. But we have suffered from balance-of-payments problems which are partly the result of our rising prices; we have allowed certain groups to suffer hardship, or at least relatively reduced their standard of living, compared with those with the skill or luck to make their way in the unusual circumstances of such a world; institutions and charities dependent on invested funds have either had to devote time and energy to a progressive investment policy, or, if apathetic, have suffered from erosion of their real income. These are serious enough problems.

If we turn to analyse the causes, there are economists who believe that if only the government were restrained enough in its monetary and fiscal policy and in cutting down its own expenditure, it could eliminate the causes of inflation, which they would ascribe to 'excessive demand'. While not disputing that excessive demand needs to be eliminated, and can be a cause of inflation, as it has been on occasions in the fifties, it is not accepted by all, or even most, economists that this explanation is adequate. It is not disputed that, if demand is cut down enough, with no regard to the degree of unemployment that will be required, then price stability can be achieved. Some might be ready to pay this price, most not. But if the treatment of excessive demand cannot thus be the sole remedy for inflation, we have to look at the processes by which, in a modern economy, we alter our incomes, and we are forced to ascribe a major influence to the processes of free collective bargaining.

We are then left with the simple conclusion that unless we can do something about the anarchic processes by which trade unions and professional associations bargain for their incomes, we are likely to suffer from the continuing curse of rising prices. It is simple arithmetic that, if the real national product per head rises by 2–3 per cent., people can only expect on average a 2–3 per cent. increase in real incomes, and that, if on average they receive more, then prices will rise correspondingly. But it is not simple to allocate the 2–3 per cent. annual increase between different groups.

The pattern of incomes cannot remain static, so that we cannot envisage a situation in which everyone gets the same increase. There are two basic factors involved. Some industries are expanding and others relatively contracting; it is natural that the expanding industries should attract labour by offering higher wages (which they are in a position to do). At the same time, the value to the community of different skills is continually altering, so that the relative differentials can hardly remain constant. Thus the society in which we live could with the greatest difficulty operate with a fixed-income structure. It is always to the advantage of a particular group to get in first, even if the result in the longer run is no net gain. Nor can we reasonably expect an incomes policy to be confined to wages, when dividends and profits are uncontrolled, when those who live on capital gains are untaxed, and when the incomes of the better-paid professional classes (doctors, university teachers, civil servants) are determined by a separate set of bargains and manipulated by *ex parte* tax concessions. A government genuinely desiring an acceptable incomes policy does not start with large tax concessions to surtax payers.

It is thus clear that a very wide range of problems is opened up once we start to work out an incomes policy, on which general agreement is hardly possible, and where at best we might hope for a precarious balance. Many economists, including myself, believe that with a higher rate of growth of the economy, and therefore a higher possible rate of growth of real wages (which does not seem at all technically impossible), the problem will be eased. Indeed, the policy of the last ten years, which has tried to solve the problems of inflation and balance-of-payments deficits by reducing the rate of growth of the economy, has almost certainly made the problem worse. Nevertheless, the problem is likely to persist. With higher rates of growth, demands may grow correspondingly, leaving the gap as before. Nor is it easy to see any simple organizational changes which will persuade trade unions or governments to abandon their traditional habits and which will make the pursuit of their normal objectives compatible with the larger aims of society.

The setting up of the National Economic Development Council, desirable as it is, will not of itself necessarily produce any solution.[25]

A second problem of a different order has been summed up in the phrase 'meritocracy'. Those who have lived in both Scotland and England will be aware that Scotland does not suffer from the traditional class differences which are a curse of English society. Without the double school system of England, and the subtle gradations of rank that make social intercourse so perilous and restricted in England, it is easier for men to talk to each other in Scotland. In principle, careers are more open to merit in Scotland. But, in practice, merit is hard to assess, and age often provides a substitute. Precisely because, in Scotland, functional positions are in principle open to merit, and in practice enjoyed by the aged, they are given a respect which they do not enjoy in a society where social hierarchies cut across functional, so that a junior can speak to his ultimate superior across his immediate superior because he has been to the same old school. A functional society, made rigid by the ascendancy of age, as in Scotland, can be more damaging than a more traditional class society. But a more scientific functional society, where merit is rewarded as fully as is practicable in human affairs, may seem even more uninspiring to those who fail to achieve the appropriate pass degree. The despair of parents at the failure of their children to pass the 11-plus reflects this malaise, and not merely because the 11-plus may not be a very efficient

[25] No doubt the collection of better statistics about wages and incomes, and more detailed study of the processes of wage bargaining will help. But it is not clear that knowledge of the facts in this field can of itself bring together groups whose interests diverge seriously.

test.[26] We may indeed expect the malaise to grow as we move further from a class-based society to a mobile society where educational attainment determines one's ultimate place in the social order.

These problems are similar: the first concerns the distribution of incomes, the second the distribution of status. Neither are soluble in principle, there being no ideal distribution, ultimately satisfactory to every group. We could indeed imagine a society where a partial solution was found by distributing incomes and status inversely, so that those with low status had high incomes and vice versa. It is indeed one of the strange assumptions of our Western world that status and income should go together. But there are few signs that such a scheme would prove acceptable.

Three fundamental problems of any society are the distribution of power, riches, and status. Political theorists have much concerned themselves with the first, and experience with the development of 'democracies' of various kinds has shown us a wide range of possible ways of controlling those with power and avoiding some of its corrupting tendencies. In the case of incomes, complete equality is possible, as it is not in the case of power. In my view we ought to move much nearer to such equality, and, as we move nearer, we can discuss how much inequality is practically convenient; I do not believe we have got within range of the point where such questions will become acute. In the case of status, for a different reason from that which applies to power, equality is also impossible. In the case of power, it is impossible to imagine an efficient society, or indeed an

[26] Research has shown how success in education for those of similar I.Q. depends a great deal on social background.

organized society at all, which does not have centres of power. It is, however, possible to imagine a society where all jobs have equal status. Indeed such an ideal lies behind much belief in democracy. As suggested earlier, it also lies behind the idea of the secular imageless society of the 'common man'. Such an ideal does not run counter to any practical requirements of social organization. It merely requires that men should not think more highly of themselves and of their social or economic position than they think of that of others, and that they do not look up to others with awe and respect merely because of their position. Such conditions do not depend only on social organization, though no doubt social organization can help, or hinder, towards such attitudes. As human societies become more mature, is it entirely idealistic to hope that men may move more in this direction? In any case, the confused complex society in which we live does at least provide a great diversity of status hierarchies which often conflict with each other.

It is quite possible that, in the case of both the concrete problems discussed earlier, things will get worse before they get better. Trade unions and professional associations show no signs of giving up their power and their consciousness of their bargaining strength may be growing. A more scientifically directed society at the same time tightens up the selection processes and entry to more and more occupations is limited to those who have passed through the official selection channels. Conflicts and resentments could grow as traditional class barriers are progressively broken down, as they surely will be.

Nevertheless, there is this to be said. We are not discussing a static pattern of incomes or status. In a changing society, new jobs come into being, and old ones cease to be useful. New skills produce new professions, and old ones lose in importance. The changes in the relative incomes of different occupations are, over fairly short periods, most startling, and similar changes occur in occupational status. One has only to point to the relative fortunes of coal-miners and ministers of religion over the last half-century. We may see more startling changes in the future. As the black-coated element grows more important in the economic structure, it is not inconceivable that trade unions, as we know them today, will become less important than other groupings in the push-and-pull of incomes. It is already arguable that the salary inflation process is as dangerous and anarchic as the wage-push element, though, at the moment, it is concerned with a much smaller slice of the national income.[27]

The mere fact of changed positions changes the roles of different groups; those resentful and discontented in one period become the boastful haves of the next. No one group need feel permanently barred from riches or status. Greater educational opportunity and social mobility will afford outlets for individual energies. Nor is it possible to conceive that a permanent hierarchy of merit can ever be enforced on such a society. If the selection process becomes too rigid, it will be by-passed by the growth of new occupations, which will not be tied to the older structures, as has happened many times in the past history of rigid professions.

These problems are difficult enough, but not so difficult as to suggest that such a society must inevitably in some

[27] The cycle of doctors—university teachers—school teachers— civil servants—university teachers, &c., does not differ from the coal-miners—engineers—railway workers—coal-miners cycle.

sense break down, or prove ultimately unsatisfying to men. The desire for riches and status have moved men in all societies, and always will; they are part and parcel of ordinary human motivation, the price of original sin. It is their excessive domination that Christians can rightly attack in a given social order. In the unpleasant vulgarity we find in our society at all levels there is much to condemn. When uncontrolled advertisement panders to these motives, we must ask for it to be limited. We can rightly demand a much higher standard than we do in fact find among our leaders today. But if we ask, as a matter of analysis, whether our society is worse than others in this respect, it is not at all clear that our vulgar drive for riches and status is more pronounced than that of medieval Italian merchants, Renaissance adventurers, Elizabethan gentry on the make, eighteenth-century nabobs, or Edwardian millionaires. It is not clear that we suffer from some 'permanent neurosis' different from that of Regency England, for example. Certainly more people are affected, partly because there are more people about, and partly because opportunities are more equal for all. Opportunities for all are much enlarged and, with them, the desire for enjoyment of what they bring. But it is not clear that people are in fact as dominated by these unsatisfiable desires as would be suggested by reading what the advertisers say or what the journalists think fit to publish. Not nearly enough attention is given to the development of simple constructive leisure activities, such as gardening, hiking, travel, which may be of more long-run importance for our culture than the more blatant absurdities of Hollywood.

The real dangers of our society, in my view, are to be found not in the changes it brings about, but rather in its failure to change quickly enough. It is not that we set our hopes too high, but that we do not set them high enough. We should fear our tawdry complacency, our contentedness that things are so good, when we should be indignant that they are not, as they could be, so much better. We are not wrong to dream of a car for everyone, but we are wrong if we fail to dream of a society where everyone could have a car and still live in civilized cities in gracious ease. We are content with slum-clearance (slow enough in all conscience), when what we need is a vision of a new Britain, building twentieth-century cities, and not merely patching up holes in the old. We are content because we have a fair and high-minded civil service, when we should be indignant that it lacks the economic and scientific expertise which is necessary to deal with the problems of the twentieth century and which it is not difficult in principle to apply to these problems.[28] We are content because British businessmen have achieved some striking results and overall have not failed us miserably, when we should be biting in our condemnation of the sheer incompetence displayed by so many well-known firms.[29] We vote for politicians because they give us something of what we want, when we should be denouncing them for their failure to lead us with imagination towards greater achievements. We are content because we are as well off as our neighbours, and our behaviour is no worse than theirs, when we should be ashamed that we do not set

[28] One might refer specifically to the failures of Whitehall to apply economic analysis to the problems of investment in the nationalized industries, as documented in the reports of the Select Committee on the Nationalized Industries.

[29] As illustrated by the failure of transformers on Glasgow suburban electric trains.

ourselves higher standards than those of the average man.

We must turn to the second question, whether in our complex specialized society we have ceased to be 'men'. There is clearly a sense in which our jobs are more specialized and our activities narrower than in previous societies. It is not certain that the horizons which bound the ordinary man are necessarily closer than those which set the limits for men in simpler societies.[30] In modern society men meet more different people of varied background. But that specialization is a necessary condition of the division of labour and hence of economic progress is clear. Can we be men if we know less and less about the affairs of men generally, and if what we do becomes a smaller and smaller part of the total product towards which our work contributes?

A university teacher can talk about his own job. He becomes more and more aware that it is impossible to have a comprehensive acquaintance with what is going on in his own special field, say economics, much less the adjoining fields of knowledge and those further areas beyond these. One becomes an expert in trade-cycle theory or public finance, with a smattering of knowledge of subjects at the periphery. If the teacher has to be a specialist, so has the taught. If a degree is not to be a test of a smattering of knowledge ten years old, but an indication that a man has some idea of the way in which people grapple at the frontiers with new ideas and with the new techniques to solve new problems, he has to go in at the deep end; some, indeed, never come out. If we have to be thus specialists, we find that conversation

[30] As I have argued in *God and the Rich Society* (O.U.P. 1961), pp. 119 f.

with others becomes difficult, and that we have few links with our opposite numbers. We yearn for the days when books were rare and there was not the flood of printed (and duplicated) matter which overwhelms us, and when men could be experts in most of the fields of human knowledge. But there is no way back. We know too much to do things in the old way, and, if the job is to be done as best we can, it must be done the new way. What is true of the field of knowledge, is also true of ordinary everyday jobs.

Poets are the outsiders of our society and it is not surprising that they should often reflect despair and despondency, and should yearn for men to be men. But we all cherish some ideal of the 'all-round man', however impossible we know it to be. We all know from experience that our capabilities do not exactly fit the groove we find ourselves in, and that we have gifts and desires that we cannot wholly exercise in our actual lives. In our leisure and our 'spare-time' activities we may to some extent find channels for these extraneous gifts, but only to some extent. Perhaps above all to be pitied are those who find in their work the complete outlet for their energies and seem to be totally given up to it : we rightly suspect them. The ordinary man is rightly dissatisfied with his lot, but this dissatisfaction is also normal. In our normal work we can never be entirely satisfied, and our frustrated energies will spill over outside our work. Nor can the rhythm of leisure provide a complete balance. There is indeed no escape from the dilemma, and never has been. The 'all-round man' is a perpetual delusion of human life.

Men are always tied to some particular and limiting concerns, and are always dissatisfied with their lot. But the attempt to be an 'all-rounder' leads to equal dissatisfaction. The desire to escape from his daily lot has been man's perpetual day-dream. In the Middle Ages it led to pilgrimages, in the eighteenth century to the Grand Tour. Literature and the arts also provide for the same needs, though, as with pilgrimages and the Grand Tour, this is not all there is to be said about the motives and reasons for our concern with these activities. But, like Lucretius's rich young man who was led by boredom to drive from his Roman flat to his country villa, but once there found life so vacant that he returned with only the shortest stay, we move between a desire to fly from our immediate circumstances and an equally strong desire to return to them. Lucretius ascribed the malaise to the fear of death—a not very plausible hypothesis.[31] Surely it is more natural to ascribe it to the dual nature of man, firmly settled in his specific physical and historical environment, and at the same time filled with yearnings for an ultimate world beyond this one. That men are threatened with a final boredom and lack of purpose is not in question—all men, and not merely intellectual or artistic *élites*. This is a human problem, not a problem of social organization; it faces every society, no doubt in different forms, but not necessarily more so today than in past ages. It is at this point that the Christian Church claims to have something to say, both to explain man to himself and to provide a pattern for his day-to-day life.

[31] *De Rerum Natura*, 3. 1053 f.

III

THE SPECIALIZED CHURCH
AND SECULAR SOCIETY

THOUGH the Christian Church has always stood for human values, it has not always seemed so to its critics, and in part they have been right. The way in which the Church has asserted human values has often seemed to deny them, and sometimes it has. At other times, it has been the Church's opponents who have failed to see how fundamental was the Church's stand. There has been a real conflict about the nature of these human values, a disagreement about what man really is. We cannot expect that those who believe that man and all the world around him are in the last resort entirely dependent on the God who made them, keeps them in existence, and redeems them, will see things in entirely the same perspective as those who believe none of these things. But the remarkable thing is how much agreement there is between the Christian view and the humanism of the West, in its modern secular form.

However much disagreement there may be about the actual Christian understanding of man, there should be none that the Christian faith in principle has always expressed its concern for man and all his works. One manifestation of this has been the development of the parochial system with the representative of Christ's Body, the persona, in each group of men. It has often been pointed out that the parson, the persona, is the representative man.

Thus Coleridge wrote of him:[1]

Persona κατ' ἐξοχήν; *persona exemplaris*; the representative and exemplar of the personal character of the community or parish; of their duties and rights, of their hopes, privileges and requisite qualifications, as moral persons, and not merely living things.

In past ages, there has been some justification for regarding the clergy as representative of all men. Today such a claim would be ludicrous. Herein lies part of our problem. In principle the Church represents all men; in practice the organized Church consists of a small group of men rather narrowly trained and highly specialized in ways remote from the life of ordinary people. The specialized Church as we know it is a denial of the reality of the Church.

The organized Church is inevitably specialized in one sense in that it is primarily concerned with preaching and the sacraments, with what goes on in church and what is tied up with it. The paid functionaries of the organization have these as their central concerns, and if these functions are to be provided we cannot do without them. If being a Christian involves worshipping in community, then these persons are required for these functions. I am not concerned with questions such as whether we could not have a half-time clergy. Whether half-time or full-time, there is a specialized function to be performed. In this sense the organized Church must in any society be specialized.

But that the clergy are specialists today in a further sense, with serious dangers in it, can hardly be doubted.

[1] Op. cit., p. 62 n.

Or perhaps it might be better to say that to the inevitable specialism has been added the professionalism that menaces any group. The clergy as professionals have no experience of other spheres of life. As professionals, they are experts in the Bible and the sacraments. As professionals, they are concerned with what goes on in Church buildings, and to attract others to be more concerned with what goes on there. As professionals, they are tempted to judge the world in terms of their own profession. They are tempted to believe that when they have spoken the words of the Bible or the Prayer Book or the textbooks of theology, they have preached the Gospel, and that it is the business of the world to learn these words. They are tempted to believe that being a Christian means participating in the activities in which clergy are active, and that the 'world' against which the Church is set consists of all those activities in which the clergy do not participate. When the clergy had a fairly clear general social function in the community as leaders of social life, they were integrated in it and they married Church and world, whether or not we are happy about the terms of the marriage. Today they have no general social function; they have no great social status; their words are not much attended to. One reaction to this changed situation is to try to justify the ghetto mentality. It can be done, not entirely unplausibly, by those who are prepared to narrow the Gospel's concern and to deny that the Church is in principle concerned with the whole world. For those who do not hold these beliefs, the problem remains.

The problem has always been with us. It is at its starkest today when a specialized Church confronts a secularized and fragmented society. We have to go back to first principles. There are three questions we have to ask. What is the relation between God and the everyday secular world? What is the relationship between theology and other subjects? What is the role of the Church in the actual world of events?

In asking what is the relationship of God to the secular world, we can approach the question from several different points of view. We can start with the hackneyed theme that the Bible is the story of God's attack on religion. Religion comes indeed from God, in that God made men capable of apprehending himself; but also it comes from men in that men, through sin, only partly apprehend him, and worship a bit of him and a bit of themselves. Religion creates a ritual, an establishment, a theology, a priesthood, a moral law. God speaks to men in and through these, and men make themselves at home in them and find them worthwhile activities on their own, regardless of God. Then God breaks them, and comes himself to men, alone, outside the establishment, denied by it, offering no alternative establishment, but something different, the simple acceptance of himself. Meanwhile the ordinary world goes on as ever.

The theme of religion against God has become fairly commonplace in the twentieth century with the awakening of interest in the works of Kierkegaard, who expressed the thesis with a wealth of imagination and a bitterness of personal frustration which repels as well as attracts. But the same theme was to be found in England, in the writings of Kingsley and Maurice. The latter expressed it thus:[2]

Religion against God. This is the heresy of our age, as

[2] *The Life of F. D. Maurice*, vol. i, p. 518, vol. ii, p. 475.

Irving said long ago,—how often have I blessed him for the words,—and this is leading to the last most terrific form of infidelity (1849).

If my Christianity, or your Christianity, or any man's Christianity stand between you or me or him and God, who is our Father, Christ who is our Brother, *He* will sweep that Christianity away. He will set you or me or him upon another kind of search, a weary one, it may be, but far more hopeful, more godly, than acquiescence in anything, which may only have concealed an unfathomable Atheism (1864).

The Bible shows a complex pattern of relationships between God and the religious world. But at least it never allows men to get away with the idea that God is only interested in religion. It is in the religious world that he finds some of his greatest enemies. On the other hand, the everyday world of ordinary work is taken for granted as part of God's world. This he made, and to this he came as a man. Not a great deal is said about it that is of much direct use to us in our daily concerns. The world has always had to go about its business without any very clear guidance about it. In so far as the Law of the Old Testament did try to provide such guidance, it was precisely this detailed guidance which was condemned by Jesus. No other guidance was offered, and what lies implicit in Old and New Testaments belongs to a small-scale world of villages and city-states and is not very helpful to us today.

There is thus a problem of Christian ethics. But there is a prior problem about God himself and his operations in the world. Men have always veered between a belief that God was breathing down their backs (or even closer than that) and a belief that he was unbelievably remote. The Christian faith does not differ, except that it firmly locates God in a man who lived in a past epoch, and whose activity it believes to be concentrated in the sacraments which he initiated, and which are linked both to the past and to that which lies beyond our world of space and time. In day-to-day life Christians have moved between the two poles of belief in the presence and absence of God as much as the adherents of other religions.

One inexcusable resolution of the inevitable tension was open to earlier generations, but is no longer available to us. This was to locate God's activities—let us call them his Providence—in certain particular spheres of life. God worked in miracles and miracles occurred regularly outside the normal framework of life. But, as the normal framework of life in a pre-scientific world was severely limited, the scope for miraculous intervention was wide, and credulity enlarged it even further. If we believe in God, we must believe he can perform miracles, but we are not inhibited from being rigorously sceptical about any alleged miracles that are reported to us. Nor do we find the presence of miracles a convincing argument for the activity of God. What appears to be a miracle may after all in due course, as knowledge grows, be interpreted otherwise, and we cannot subject the events of past credulous epochs to the tests we would apply today. Jesus' refusal to produce overwhelming 'signs' as conclusive proof of his status appeals to us as more true to the nature of God as we see him than the proofs from miracles which appealed to many earlier generations of theologians.

The Bible asserts that God is active in his world. No doubt this was interpreted in many different ways, but the way of miraculous intervention was always one that produced an immediate appeal to men. In the course of the development of history in the Christian West men learned to look at the world scientifically and in beginning to understand how things actually came about were less impressed by the apparent irregularities that were formerly called miracles. God was then relegated to direct operation on the events as yet not fully understood or explained in a scientific fashion—earthquakes, the weather, complex economic phenomena.

When the eighteenth-century Enlightenment drove theologians from trust in miracles, they turned to trust in a narrower sphere of Providence, where God manifested himself in the guidance of individual lives. It was the achievement of the Evangelical Movement to give reality in countless lives to this belief, and it handed this belief on to the leaders of the Oxford Movement, who were more dominated by the ethos of Evangelicalism than they were tempted to admit. The individualistic moralism of Evangelical piety was deeply ingrained in their thinking, and dominated most of the religion of the High Victorian era. Here God was allowed to work his Providence out. Beyond this narrow field God was conceived as encouraging the British nation to develop its mission to the world. In other words, Providence in the personal field was a creative force; in the social field it provided glorification for the *status quo*. This unhelpful dichotomy was used even by some critics of the *status quo*.[3]

But for twentieth-century man God cannot thus be relegated to the personal field. For two reasons. Firstly,

---

[3] Thus we find more than a trace of it in F. D. Maurice, who transcended the nineteenth century more than most theologians of his time.

we do not believe in a God who is only interested in the personal sphere. We have learnt too well from F. D. Maurice, Westcott, Gore, Temple, and others who have recalled us to the true nature of the Gospel. But, secondly, one ground for the conviction of God's action in the personal sphere has been taken away from us. We have discovered that the personal sphere is as subject to scientific laws as the outside world and the realm of social behaviour.

The nineteenth century showed that a science of human society was possible, and the development of economics and sociology made rapid advances. It was left to the end of the century and the first half of the next for science to invade man's private personal life. With the advent of Freud the special interventions of God in private life become as odd explanations of human behaviour as they are in the case of earthquakes. There is no field left where we can exclude science and intrude God as an alternative explanation.

The conclusion is clear. God does not provide explanations of events as does science, whether physical, social, or psychological sciences are in question. We are not to look for the hand of God in any particular fields of experience. He is in all or in none. Providence is universal or nowhere. It does not provide an explanation that we can fall back upon when other explanations fail. The battles that were fought in the nineteenth century over historical criticism and evolution, and which are sometimes fought today over analytical psychology or sociological analysis, are fundamentally absurd. The tools that these inquiries have provided for us, as well as those provided by philosophers in the analysis of language, are necessary and fundamental parts of our everyday life.

There can be no conflict in principle between their use and the glory of God. The world they reveal to us has always been there, and it is God's world; the use of these tools is no different in principle from the use of simpler tools by primitive societies, or the more sophisticated tools already available to men in the days of faith.

The questions we have to ask about God's relation to his everyday world lie deeper. It has always been men's desire to find God somewhere easily at hand; but men have never had much success in their endeavours. Nor does the Incarnation of itself provide an easy revelation of God. Jesus refused the temptation to overwhelm men by an overbearing miracle, or to crush them with supernatural power. Instead the Son of Man emptied himself, and was hidden among the ordinary ways of men. The New Testament swings between the dogmatic assertion that 'God is clearly here' and the hesitant doubt that he is hiding himself that men's faith may be proved; seeing is very different from believing.

The shrill note of certainty is frequently an excuse for an inner uncertainty and so it has often been in Christian history. When men are honest, again and again there rings out the cry to the God who hides himself, and is not clearly to be seen among his people. On the one hand, the psalmist writes of God's closeness: 'Thou compassest my path and my lying down, and art acquainted with all my ways. . . . Whither shall I go from thy spirit? or whither shall I flee from thy presence?' But, on the other hand, he also cries to God: 'Hide not thy face from me.'[4] So St. John can write that 'No man hath seen God at any time,' as well as 'He that hath seen me hath seen the Father'.[5] So, too, the New Testament finds its most

[4] Psalms 139. 3, 7; 102, 2.   [5] 1. 18; 14. 9.

profound note in the cry 'My God, my God, why hast thou forsaken me?'.[6]

Even St. Bernard with all his determination and certainty could write:[7]

We have to seek for purely spiritual reasons why He Who says 'Seek, and ye shall find' and 'He that seeketh findeth' yet cannot be found. . . . It is night always when we look for Him; for, were it day, He would reveal Himself and we should have no need to seek. . . . Believe, and you have found Him; for finding and believing are the same.

So, too, his friend William of St. Thierry:[8]

Why hidest Thou Thy Face? Dost Thou account me as Thine enemy? . . . And I, Lord, know not whither I am travelling, and how can I know the way?

So again the fourteenth-century English mystic Walter Hilton:[9]

There is no need to travel to Rome or Jerusalem to search for Him: but turn your thoughts into your own soul where He is hidden, and seek Him there. For as the prophet says: 'Vere tu es deus absconditus' [Isa. xlv. 15]. Truly, Lord, Thou art a hidden God.

The classic sixteenth-century Spanish mystics had a great deal to say about the dark night of the soul, but the same point is made in more everyday terms by those whose

[6] Matthew xxvii. 46.
[7] *On the Song of Songs*, translated by A Religious of C.S.M.V. (Mowbrays, 1952), pp. 233–8.
[8] *The Meditations of William of St. Thierry*, by the same (Mowbrays, 1954), pp. 76–77.
[9] *The Ladder of Perfection*, translated by L. Sherley-Price (Penguin, 1957), p. 61.

advice was for people living in the world. Thus Fénélon could write: [10]

Blessed are they who lack everything, even the conscious perception and experience of God Himself. Blessed are they from whom Jesus is hidden and withdrawn. The Holy Ghost, the Comforter, will come to them. . . . Awareness of the absence of the Saviour and all His gifts attracts the Holy Ghost.

And again an eighteenth-century Jesuit: [11]

The way of love is a way of faith, and is, consequently, dark and obscure; and this is exactly where the merit lies. In it we must walk blindfold, without knowing where we are or whither God is leading us.

We do not need to go back so far in history or to other countries. We find the same point made even in the full flush of Victorian conviction, which seems so remote from our world in so many respects. Thus Dean Church preached on prayer: [12]

Does it never come into your thoughts how strange a thing it is that One whom we talk of so much, we never see, we never can see here, no man has ever seen? No one has ever seen God. . . . He is a hidden God, though the world could not last a moment unless He was close at hand. We talk of Him, think of Him, know that He is there; but no sign does He ever give, no message now comes from Him, His voice never speaks aloud. . . . We must speak, but we get no answer which mortal ears can hear. . . . We receive

[10] *Meditations and Devotions*, selected and translated by E. C. Fenn, (Mowbrays, 1954), pp. 54–55.

[11] *Meditations on the Love of God*, by Father Nicholas Grou, S.J., translated by the Benedictines of Teignmouth (Burns Oates and Washbourne, 1948), p. 144.

[12] *Village Sermons*, Second Series (1894), pp. 221–2, 224–5.

no sign, that we can make certain of, of the answering love of God. . . . By faith only, not by sight, can we attain to, or enjoy, the knowledge of God.

The relevance of this common note of many Christian writers through the ages is that it makes us face more clearly the fact that there is no separate sphere of 'religion' where God is to be found. If there is no such separate sphere, if God is a hidden God, he is equally a God who is everywhere in the ordinary everyday world. Thus Dean Church relates how the Oxford Movement followed the pattern of the Roman schools. 'The distinction between the secular life and the life of "religion", with all its consequences, became an accepted one.'[13] With all its consequences! In principle, Maurice gave the reply:[14]

'He is in you. He is the source of all the good deeds you have ever done, of all the good thoughts you have ever thought; He it is who has resisted all the evil that you have ever been tempted to do.' May not we clergymen have been hiding this gospel from our fellow-creatures, preaching a certain job-divinity, certain things about Christ—not Christ Himself, the Head of every man, the Deliverer of mankind from sin, death, the grave, hell?

And so he refused to make a clear distinction between belief and unbelief. As he preached in his farewell sermon in 1869 to the congregation of the chapel in Vere St.:[15]

And therefore I have not ventured, although I have felt the temptation as much as any one could, to draw a line between one class of men and another, to call those on

[13] *The Oxford Movement* (1892), p. 369.
[14] *Life*, vol. ii, p. 448.
[15] Ibid., p. 594.

this side of the line righteous or believers, those on the other side of the line unrighteous or unbelievers. . . . *I* must take my portion with the unrighteous and unbelievers; for I am conscious of an unrighteousness and an unbelief in myself which I cannot be conscious of in another. These are my foes.

If these hints give us part of the truth about God and his relations with the everyday world, we can welcome the Enlightenment and the growth of 'secularism' for making us see more clearly what is involved in the tremendous Christian claim. It is usual to denounce secularism, even if a secular society is in some sense applauded.[16] But need we go so far? Those who believe in the Christian faith believe that those who do not share their beliefs are wrong and fail to appreciate the full glory of human life. It may be that for most people there is no resting-place in a lack of faith, though we meet many around us of whom this does not seem to be true. The Christian claim differs from that of the pure secularist, not in a belief that the secularist has failed to understand one part of life—religion, nor in a necessarily different moral code in everyday matters. It differs in the belief in God, who exists 'behind' the world, and on whom it depends. The secular world has its limited aims, and God respects these; there are no other alternative aims for Christians in their everyday life. But Christians, believing in God, can see these aims as *limited*, precisely because they look for *ultimate* satisfaction to God alone.

What then of secular society? The Christian faith reveals the inexhaustible patience of God with men,

[16] See the earlier quotations from the Thessalonica Conference of the World Council of Churches. Mr. Eliot refers to 'those who can see that a thoroughgoing secularism would be objectionable' (op. cit., p. 25).

because God cares for the freedom of human choice. The more choices men have to exercise, the more responsibility is thrust upon them. A secular society enlarges the area of men's choices, and calls men to greater maturity, as Bonhoeffer has made clear to us.[17] Do men really want it? Can they bear it? It is surely the business of the organized Church and of all its members to help men to bear it, and not to call them back to childhood. I return later to the question as to what is required of the Church in this respect.

Our second question concerns the relationship between theology and other subjects. Until fairly recently it would have been agreed among theologians of the most varied views that theology was the ground of the other sciences, without whose illumination they would become perverted, distorted, and incapable of discovering the truth they were rightly concerned with. Perhaps the most brilliant exposition of this view is to be found in Newman's lectures (1852) *On the Scope and Nature of University Education*:[18]

What results of philosophic speculation are unquestionable, if they have been gained without inquiry as to what Theology had to say to them? Does it cast no light upon history? has it no influence upon the principles of ethics? is it without any sort of bearing on physics, metaphysics, and political science? Can we drop it out of the circle of knowledge, without allowing, either that that circle is thereby mutilated, or on the other hand, that Theology is no science? . . . To withdraw Theology from the public schools is to impair the completeness and to invalidate the trustworthiness of all that is actually taught in them.

[17] *Letters and Papers from Prison* by D. Bonhoeffer (1953).
[18] Everyman ed., pp. 58, 61.

A little later Pusey outlined the same point of view at Oxford.[19]

All things must speak of God, refer to God, or they are atheistic. History, without God, is a chaos without design, or end, or aim. Political Economy, without God, would be a selfish teaching about the acquisition of wealth, making the larger portion of mankind animate machines for its production; Physics, without God, would be but a dull enquiry into certain meaningless phenomena; Ethics, without God, would be a varying rule, without principle, or substance, or centre, or regulating hand; Metaphysics, without God, would make man his own temporary god, to be resolved, after his brief hour here, into the nothingness out of which he proceeded. All sciences may do good service, if those who cultivate them know their place, and carry them not beyond their sphere . . . all will tend to exclude the thought of God, if they are not cultivated with reference to Him.

We note that Pusey talks of God rather than of Theology, as did Newman, but his concern is equally about 'speaking of God' rather than with the relationship between God Himself and these subjects. It is one thing to say that Physics could not exist without God; it is another thing to say that Physics becomes a dull meaningless inquiry when it is discussed apart from discussion of God. The distinction was made by a theologian who bridges the gap between the pre-critical world of Pusey and the twentieth century and its concerns, but who was still a child of his own age—I refer to F. D. Maurice:[20]

[19] *Collegiate and Professorial Teaching and Discipline: in Answer to Prof. Vaughan's Strictures* (Oxford, 1854). Quoted in *Life of E. B. Pusey*, by H. P. Liddon (1894), vol. iii, p. 389.

[20] *Life*, vol. i, pp. 372–3; vol. ii, pp. 136–7, 311. In 1866 he talked of 'recognizing theology as the permanent ground, and the con-

If once the teachers in our theological schools would have courage to proclaim theology to be the knowledge of God and not the teaching of a religion, I am satisfied that the scientific character of the Bible would be brought out as conspicuously as its practical character. . . . Then it would not be necessary to assert for theology its place as the *scientia scientiarum,* or to bid others fall into their places in connection with it and subordination to it. . . . The truths concerning God would be felt so essential to the elucidation of those concerning men and nature, the relation of one to the other would be so evident . . . that the opposition to them would be recognized as proceeding just as much from prejudice and ignorance . . . as the opposition to gravitation or any of the most acknowledged physical or mathematical principles (1844).

My own deep conviction that theology is not (as the schoolmen have represented it) the climax of all studies, the Corinthian capital of a magnificent edifice, composed of physics, politics, economics, and connecting them as parts of a great system with each other—but is the foundation upon which they all stand. And even that language would have left my meaning open to a very great, almost an entire, misunderstanding, unless I could exchange the name theology for the name GOD, and say that He Himself is the root. . . . I fear all economics, politics, physics, are in danger of becoming Atheistic: not when they are worst, but even when they are best; that Mill, Fourier, Humboldt, are more in danger of making a system which shall absolutely exclude God, and suffice without Him, than any less faithful and consistent thinkers (1852).

I maintain on St. John's authority . . . that the knowledge of God . . . is the foundation of all knowledge of men and of things (1857).

summation of thought and life in this day' (pp. 553–4). See also vol. ii, p. 247.

In assessing these attitudes we must not forget the moral and practical fervour of many Christians of the middle of the nineteenth century, which tended to distrust learning for its own sake, and regarded universities as places for the training of the young. Thus Pusey's idea of a university was:[21]

not how to advance science, not how to make discoveries, not to form new schools of mental philosophy, nor to invent new modes of analysis; not to produce works in Medicine, Jurisprudence, or even Theology; but to form minds religiously, morally, intellectually, which shall discharge aright whatever duties God, in His Providence, shall appoint to them.

In this Pusey was in agreement with his bitter theological enemy, Jowett, and with Campbell Tait, the Archbishop of Canterbury, who in the House of Lords in 1882 stated that 'he could not help feeling that some of these professorships were more ornamental than useful', a view of learning held by a more recent holder of the same See.[22] On the other side at Oxford, there was Mark Pattison, who opposed Jowett on 'the fundamental question of university politics—viz. Science and Learning v. Schoolkeeping.[23]

[21] Op. cit., p. 390.
[22] Quoted in V. H. H. Green, *Oxford Common Room: a Study of Lincoln College and Mark Pattison* (1957), p. 258. See the quotation from Archbishop Fisher in *God and the Rich Society*, p. 157.
[23] Green, op. cit., p. 260. The issue is not dead today, though few would subscribe to the extreme view of Pusey. It is interesting to note that it was combined with fears of the introduction of the lodging-house system at Oxford, which Pusey shared with Archbishop Whately and Frederick Temple. 'This recommendation of the Commissioners [of the 1850's] is perilous in every way. It is injurious intellectually, dangerous morally, a loss religiously. It would introduce all the evils of the purely professorial system.' To which Mark

Thus, it was not perhaps surprising that, in the university of those days, elections to Chairs were dependent on theological rectitude rather than on any contribution to learning. When there were elections in 1868 for the Chairs of Poetry and Political Economy Mark Pattison commented that 'it is scarcely credible, but it is a fact, that the chances of the respective candidates are depending not on their fitness for the office, on their reputation, or past services, but on the support or opposition of the great theological party, which knows of no merit but adhesion to its ranks'.[24] So also, back in 1836, F. D. Maurice consented to stand for the Chair of Political Economy, finding that 'there was no one else ready to come forward on this ground, that political economy is not the foundation of morals and politics, but must have them for its foundation or be worth nothing', and, knowing nothing of political economy, was yet prepared to 'endeavour to master the details of the subject'.[25] But when the support of the Tractarians was withdrawn, he withdrew his candidacy. Nor does there seem any evidence that he ever took steps to 'master the details of the subject'—to his own great loss, and that of the causes he sponsored.

Coleridge belonged to a wider world than mid-century

Pattison replied: 'It is to be feared that the moral and religious standard with which a well-disposed youth comes up from a pious home, would not be elevated by close and habitual intercourse with the Senior Common Room. . . . If little or nothing of moral influence is obtained by intramural residence, neither is the College gate any mechanical security against dissolute habits.' (Quoted in *Oxford University Gazette*, 4 Dec. 1961, p. 366.) J. Tuckwell (*Reminiscences of Oxford*, 2nd ed. 1907) shows that Oxford was not quite so clerically minded as these quotations might suggest.

[24] Green, op. cit., p. 243.

[25] Op. cit., vol. i, p. 210; see also pp. 213, 222.

Oxford, and was not limited by the narrow inhibitions of the Tractarians. He had a grander vision of education and human science. His clerisy included men of all subjects, but 'the theological' was 'placed at the head of all; and of good right did it claim the precedence'.[26]

The science of theology was the root and the trunk of the knowledges that civilised man, because it gave unity and the circulating sap of life to all other sciences. . . . To divinity belong those fundamental truths, which are the common ground-work of our civil and our religious duties, not less indispensable to a right view of our temporal concerns, than to a rational faith respecting our immortal well-being. Not without celestial observations can even terrestrial charts be accurately constructed.

So again Mr. Eliot reverted to the theme.[27] In a Christian society, 'the educational system will be formed according to Christian presuppositions of what education —as distinct from mere instruction—is for. . . . Education must be religious . . . in the sense that its aims will be directed by a Christian philosophy of life.' No longer, in contrast to Coleridge's day, 'can the supremacy of the theologian be either expected or imposed in the same way'. Indeed, he commented on the specialization that had invaded theology:[28]

Just as those who should be the intellectuals regard theology as a special study, like numismatics or heraldry, with which they need not concern themselves, and theo-

[26] Op. cit., pp. 55–57. Much of what he says, it is to be noted, refers specifically to the past.

[27] Op. cit., pp. 36–37. Mr. Eliot was much concerned with 'the necessity for criteria and values' (p. 75), and a common background of knowledge (p. 38).

[28] p. 40.

logians observe the same indifference to literature and art, as special studies which do not concern *them*, so our political classes regard both fields as territories of which they have no reason to be ashamed of remaining in complete ignorance.

But how can we expect this mutual concern to operate in our specialized world?

It is clear that we can expect little help from the theologians. There may be a theology which could be written today to speak to the men of the twentieth century; but it does not seem that our theologians are equipped to write it. They have made their subject academically respectable at the expense of making it unusable for the ordinary educated man, much less the man in the street. In this they are no different from those in other subjects where the pressures of expanding knowledge and new techniques make communication difficult. In all subjects there is need for intelligent vulgarization, and any university which entirely fails to provide for this fails in part of its role. But this is certainly not the only role of a university nor perhaps even its main role, though certain universities may concentrate more in this direction than others. It is indeed the glory of my own university, Oxford, that, though it can claim achievements in the field of pure research that are not inferior to those of other institutions, it has also never forgotten the need for such vulgarization, or what might less offensively be called general education.

There is a place for vulgarization, but there is also a place for specialization. It is doubtful if there is any one combination of the two that will provide a universal recipe. If some people are to be trained as specialists—and if we do not do that, we cannot expect to advance knowledge—then they will have to find the balance between their own subject and others by exploration at the margins of their own subject. One may be sceptical whether such balance is found by making physicists read Shakespeare or students of literature study atoms. But if a study of physics spills over into interest in the use of similar mathematical tools by, for example, economists, and a study of Shakespeare leads to a study of Renaissance art, then people are enriched in their lives and begin to grasp something of the pattern of human knowledge. Even where we are not training specialists, we cannot give students some general survey of knowledge which ignores the fact that knowledge is made up of the contribution of particular specialisms. There is no universal body of knowledge today that can be grasped by one man.[29] None of which precludes the creation of suitable general degree courses at some universities, with new combinations of subjects; but this can in the nature of the case only form part of the general solution. Mr. Eliot's preference for a 'common background of knowledge'[30] can be taken as both impracticable and undesirable in a world of the complexity of ours. We have to put up with the confusion of our complexity, and find stimulus in it as we can.

If there can be no 'common background of knowledge', there can equally be no commonly-held set of intellectual principles. There can be no other place for theology than as one subject among the rest. Just as God has been

[29] If there is no universal body of knowledge today, it is equally the case that we are not faced with 'Two Cultures'. There are almost as many cultures as there are subjects. Nor is it a helpful division to distinguish 'science' from 'arts' subjects, thus ignoring both the social sciences and the wide gap between theoretical and applied sciences.   [30] Op. cit., p. 38.

eliminated from any special corners of the universe, in which he might be supposed to find a special home, so theology has been eliminated as a special subject which illuminates all others and without which they remain imperfect. Nothing takes its place. Philosophers would make no such claim today for their detailed careful analysis of language. Indeed it is only among the backswoodsmen and the new hierophants occasionally to be found studying literature and physical science that we find any attempt to make such claims. In the case of literature, it is perhaps a natural reflection of the fact that their subject seems of all subjects the most remote and ineffective as an intellectual discipline. In the case of science, such claims are a hangover from the days when scientists were persecuted by the followers of other disciplines in the name of these same principles. Theologians today rarely put forward even limited claims; they prefer a discreet silence, which allows them to continue undisturbed with their studies.

In the field of knowledge as in life generally, we have to find our way without the guidance of overruling principles. We come then to our third problem, that of the place of the organized Church in the specialized secular society of today, and the role of the clergy in particular. Let me first state that I see no way through this problem in terms of the solutions outlined by Coleridge and Eliot, with the 'clerisy' of the one or the 'Community of Christians' of the other. Mr. Eliot describes his more flexible group as 'a body of indefinite outline; composed of both clergy and laity, of the more conscious, more spiritually and intellectually developed of both'.[31] Both Coleridge and Eliot were deeply

[31] Op. cit., p. 42.

concerned with education and its relation to the Christian faith. Thus Eliot writes:

It will be their identity of belief and aspiration, their background of a common system of education and a common culture, which will enable them to influence and be influenced by each other, and collectively to form the conscious mind and the conscience of the nation.

But it is impossible to foresee such a 'common system of education' and 'common culture' in the world of divided beliefs in which we live. It would be better, in my view, to accept the reality of our divisions and build our society on them. This applies to education as to other fields. A society which consciously tries to provide a framework where men of different allegiances can live together in harmony need not try to paper over the cracks and pretend to agreement where in reality there is no agreement. It is clear that in such a society we can at best expect rival 'clerisies', and such, of course, we find without special provision being made for them.

One objection to the idea of a 'clerisy' is that it exaggerates the importance to society of the teacher and pastor. This is one form of professional leadership, but only one. If we look out towards a wider society, we know that the Church exists where its ordinary members exist, as they live out their ordinary lives from day to day 'in the place where God has set them'. If we widen the clerisy to include all the lay members of Christian churches, we are forced to look again at the organized Church in its relations with its ordinary members.

It is perhaps a commonplace that the laity is the Church, and that centuries of subordination of laymen to the clergy have distorted our ideas of its proper organization. May I recall to you some passages from an article by the Rev. T. R. Morton, of the Iona Community, entitled 'Is the Church clergy-ridden?'[32]

The minister has become the greatest obstacle to the development of the congregation into responsible, adult life. . . . It is taken for granted that the minister should be the arbiter of the congregation's thoughts and life. . . . Today in the absence of any effective teaching on vocation the only thing that the member can do is to take the minister as his model. . . . Where he can follow the example of the minister is in those parts of life which are common to both—the personal, domestic sides of life. So this private side of life is seen as the one plane in which the Christian life is lived. . . . The minister, by choice and profession, tends not to identify himself with controversial questions. He is often wrong in this detachment but it is understandable. The loss is not so much in the contribution he fails to make as in the impression he gives to his people that this detachment is a higher Christian virtue than active participation. And when an example calls for inaction it is generally followed.

So, too, three leading laymen spoke to the Assembly of the World Council of Churches at New Delhi:[33]

Christ is not imprisoned in our churches. Christ is *incognito* already present in the structures and power systems in which we have to live our Christian life. . . .
We sometimes have the feeling that you have little understanding for this our solidarity with our non-Christian neighbours and colleagues, because your professional concern is so much concentrated on the Church when it is assembled for corporate worship, witness and service. You

[32] *Frontier* (Summer 1961), pp. 127–30.
[33] 'The Laity: The Church in the World', by Klaus von Bismarck, E. V. Mathew, and Mollie Batten (*Ecumenical Review*, Jan. 1962).

often press us to become quite consciously the light of the world, to be known as Christians, to form Christian cells in the world of our work and neighbourhoods. Often such reminders are quite necessary. But more often our Christian obedience demands us to remain *incognito* and thus to serve Christ. It may then happen that suddenly, to the amazement of our non-Christian friends, the light of Christ reflects itself in us. It is then not our work but his, not our light but his.

So, too, Professor W. N. Pittenger wrote recently:[34]

God is knowable in many areas, places, and times, through what I think we may properly call *incognitos*. . . . God chooses and uses secular *incognitos*. . . . It is simply wrong, it is even blasphemous, for us to seek to break down, or break through, the *incognitos* which God thus assumes. It is precisely in and under those *incognitos*, in their very secularity, that at that time and in that given area of human activity, God is to be adored.

If we ask what this means in terms of organizations, it means clearly a redirection of the efforts of the organized Church away from Church-centred activities and towards lay institutes and centres where ordinary people can discuss their everyday problems, Christians and others together, and learn what is the proper pattern of 'active participation' in the various activities that make up society. It is to this field that I would devote the resources which the Church of England at the moment concentrates on maintaining an antiquated system of church schools. We are far behind what has been done by the churches in Germany. The clergy will have their part to play, but the Church will no longer appear to the

[34] 'Secular Study and Christian Faith' (*Theology*, Feb. 1962).

world to be the clergy's organization, as it will cease to be clergy-dominated. The Church will be seen, if seen at all, in the thick of ordinary life. So Maurice wrote of his ideal of a Working College:[35]

I have felt that a Working College, if it is to do anything, must be in direct hostility to the Secularists—that is to say, must assert that as its foundation principle which they are denying. But to do this effectually it must also be in direct hostility to the Religionists—that is to say, it must assert the principle that God is to be sought and honoured in every pursuit, not merely in something technically called religion.

We might be more welcoming today to secularism; there is no great gulf between men who share a sensitive respect for human values; in any case we have to work together in society. What we have to find is the true vocation of the Christian in the world today. When Christians have developed their own pattern of living in contemporary terms, then in their everyday lives they may become salt and savour to others. They may then guide others as a 'clerisy', because others copy them, whether knowing it or not.

When finally we look at all this world of politics and economics with all its organizations and various activities from the standpoint of Christian faith, what does it all amount to? We are called to be saints; what then is the proper pattern of sanctity in this world of politics and people?

We are not saints, but we are 'called to be saints'.[36] The grace of God works in us to make us saints; what

[35] Op. cit., vol. ii, p. 319.   [36] Romans i. 7.

will become of us we do not know, nor need we worry; we are in God's hands. But let us not in our blindness set limits to God's grace and to the glorious destiny to which he calls us. Let us not narrow down the glory of God to the pettiness of our own minds. Let us not fill ourselves with such a narrow conception of what it is to be a Christian that people will say that Christians have not even appreciated the grandeur of man's achievement; if we have not appreciated the grandeur of man, how can we adore God whom we have not seen? Our Lord and Master Jesus Christ humbled himself to become a man:[37] all our human achievements were shown to be naught at the foot of his Cross. And this does not mean that God does not care for our human achievements, and dismisses them with contempt; it means precisely the opposite, that this grandeur is so great that in its light our greatness appears tawdry and shoddy. Nor does it mean that we must disentangle ourselves from the world; it means rather that we must entangle ourselves the more, because there God is to be found. And so as Christians we land up exactly where we started, in the same world as everybody else, not saved *from* it, but in process of being saved *in* it, and spending our time saving it, 'redeeming the time'[38] and all that takes place in time. But now we know that nothing can 'separate us from the love of God which is in Christ Jesus'.[39] And we know that 'It is finished'[40]—the great work of redemption. In the words of the traditional liturgy for Easter Saturday, 'This is the night that . . . hath purged away the darkness of iniquity. . . . O night truly blessed. . . . O night wherein heavenly things are joined unto earthly, things human

---

[37] Philippians ii. 8.   [38] Ephesians v. 16.
[39] Romans viii. 39.   [40] John xix. 30.

unto things divine.' And, so, because the man Jesus Christ rose from the dead after having suffered on the Cross, human things are for ever made part of God. And nothing shall put asunder that union of man and God—not even the perversity of Christians.

PRINTED IN GREAT BRITAIN
AT THE UNIVERSITY PRESS, OXFORD
BY VIVIAN RIDLER
PRINTER TO THE UNIVERSITY